What to Expect in the Military

★ ★ ★ ★ ★

A Practical Guide for Young People, Parents, and Counselors

P. J. Budahn

GREENWOOD PRESS
Westport, Connecticut • London

Library of Congress Cataloging-in-Publication Data

Budahn, P. J. (Phillip J.), 1949–
    What to expect in the military : a practical guide for young people, parents, and
    counselors / P. J. Budahn.
        p. cm.
    Includes bibliographical references and index.
    ISBN 0–313–31003–3 (alk. paper)
        1. United States—Armed Forces—Vocational guidance. I. Title.
UB323.B766 2000
355'.0023'73—dc21   00–025678

British Library Cataloguing in Publication Data is available.

Copyright © 2000 by P. J. Budahn

Library of Congress Catalog Card Number: 00–025678
ISBN: 0–313–31003–3

First published in 2000

Greenwood Press, 88 Post Road West, Westport, CT 06881
An imprint of Greenwood Publishing Group, Inc.
www.greenwood.com

Printed in the United States of America

∞™

The paper used in this book complies with the
Permanent Paper Standard issued by the National
Information Standards Organization (Z39.48–1984).

10 9 8 7 6 5 4 3 2 1

CONTENTS

PREFACE

As the nation moves into a new century, the number of men and women who have served in the armed forces is, sadly, decreasing. These old warriors, some still showing up in their blue American Legion caps for patriotic events, others quietly going about their lives, once played an important role in helping young people decide to walk into a military recruiter's office for the first time.

For me, being in the military for a couple years during the waning days of the Vietnam War wasn't tough. The difficult part was deciding whether I wanted to enter that strange world of uniforms and salutes and parades.

Like more than 200,000 Americans every year, I made the decision to join, and as the years pass I look back on that time in the military as one of the most interesting periods of my life.

What to Expect in the Military was written to give young people the sort of practical insights into the military that I picked up naturally in a time when a large percentage of adult men were veterans of World War II.

This isn't a recruiting tract. It's a straightforward account of the process of being in the military, starting with recruiters, going through boot camps, and ending with details about the military's retirement program.

Although I slip into the second-person pronoun frequently, as if the reader were a young person thinking about enlisting, this volume was composed to be helpful to parents, guidance counselors, even former veterans who aren't sure about the changes that have come to the armed forces since they took off their uniforms.

I've tried to be sensitive to matters of gender and avoid pronouns that make it seem that only men are in the military. When faced with the choice of being clear or sensitive, I chose clarity. When I have written about re-servists, I also include members of the National Guard.

Many people made this book possible. Most of them were only a year or two into their military tours. I've included a list of all the people who helped in the acknowledgments section of this book. To them, I am grate-ful. To the young men and women who will step into the ranks of the armed forces in the future, prepared to do the nation's business wherever duty calls, all of us are grateful.

ACKNOWLEDGMENTS

The author wishes to thank the dozens of people who contributed their personal stories or their professional expertise to this book. Without their interest and support, this book would not have been possible. Of course, any errors are solely the responsibility of the author.

The interviewees included: 2d Lt. Jessica Acosta, Tehachapi, Calif. (Marine Corps, Quantico, Va.); Sgt. Stephen Allen, Dallas (Marine Corps, Quantico, Va.); Pvt. Tony Baker, Greenville, Ohio (Army, Fort Knox, Ky.); Sr. Airman Rickie Banister, Eastern Shore (Langley Air Force Base, Va.); AN Jayson Bates, Eugene, Ore. (USS *Harry S. Truman*); ST3 George Benecke, Brooklyn, N.Y. (USS *Oklahoma City*); Pvt. Brady Beyer, Salt Lake City, Utah (Army, Fort Knox, Ky.); Lance Cpl. Eric Brodecki, Bensalen, Pa. (Marine Corps, Quantico, Va.); PFC Mike Campbell, High Point, N.C. (Army, Fort Knox, Ky.); Staff Sgt. Martin Celestine, Jr., St. Thomas, Virgin Islands (Fort Benning, Ga.) and Lance Cpl. Danette Cruz, New York City (Marine Corps, Quantico, Va.).

Also interviewed were Sr. Airman Rachel Cunningham, Cleveland (Langley Air Force Base, Va.); Staff Sgt. Jeffery Day, Detroit (Langley Air Force Base, Va.); Pvt. Terrence Edward, Chicago, Ill. (Army, Fort Knox, Ky.); SA Matthew Flynn, Severna Park, Md. (Coast Guard, St. Inigoes, Md.); Lance Cpl. Andrew Fulda, Columbia, Md. (Marine Corps, Quantico, Va.); Master Sgt. Ronald Graves, Jarratt, Va. (Langley Air Force Base, Va.); Sgt. 1st Class Stanley Griffin, Fayetteville, N.C. (Army, Fort Knox, Ky.); SSG Kenneth Hignight, Radcliff, Ky. (Army, Fort Knox, Ky.); AK3 Jason Hodges, Washington, N.C. (Norfolk Naval Station, Va.); Lt. Cmdr. Nancy

Holcome, Dixon, Ill. (Spokane, Wash.); and ET3 Thomas Knowland, Maple Shade, N.J. (USS *Oklahoma City*).

Thanks to interviewees Pvt. Cory Livingstone, Conway, S.C. (Army, Fort Knox, Ky.); Lance Cpl. Brian McElaney, Sharon Hills, Pa. (Marine Corps, Quantico, Va.); Airman 1st Class Trevor McIntyre, Waldorf, Md. (Langley Air Force Base, Va.); Spec. Kenneth Morin, Providence, R.I. (Army, Fort Knox, Ky.); Airman 1st Class Susan Nichols, Denver, Colo. (Langley Air Force Base, Va.); Pvt. Brian Norton, Dylan, S.C. (Army, Fort Knox, Ky.); PN2 Mauricia Porter, Meridian, Miss. (USS *Harry S. Truman*); Staff Sgt. Derek Presley, Perry, Okla. (Army, Fort Knox, Ky.); Capt. Bryan Salmon, Colorado Springs, Colo. (Langley Air Force Base, Va.); Pvt. Scott Smith, Onarga, Ill. (Army, Fort Knox, Ky.); and Pvt. Joshua Thorn, Petoskey, Mich. (Army, Fort Knox, Ky.).

Also interviewed were Cpl. Kelly Torres, Benton, Ill. (Marine Corps, Quantico, Va.); Spec. Germinie Turner, Alexandria, Va. (Army, Fort Knox, Ky.); Pvt. Jason Victory, Standing Stone, Pa. (Army, Fort Knox, Ky.); Pvt. Mark Wakefield, West Valley, Utah (Army, Fort Benning); Cpl. Judson Yerkes, Jacksonville, Fla. (Marine Corps, Quantico, Va.); and Cpl. Jose Zepeda, Roswell, N.M. (Marine Corps, Quantico, Va.).

Thanks also to the people who helped arrange interviews, found data, got copies of reports, or who did all of the above and more, including Lt. Erin Bradley, Langley Air Force Base, Va.; Bill Carlson, U.S. Coast Guard, Cape May, N.J.; Capt. Shawn Clemons, U.S. Marine Corps, Quantico, Va.; Lt. Toni Gay, U.S. Coast Guard, Baltimore, Md.; Maj. Joseph Hampton, Fort Knox, Ky.; Ray Harp, Army Training and Doctrine Command, Fort Monroe, Va.; Lt. Cmdr. Cedric Hughes, U.S. Coast Guard Recruiting Center; Elsie Jackson, Fort Benning, Ga.; Ens. Mark Jones, Naval Training Command, Great Lakes, Ill.; and Lt. Denise Kerr, Lackland Air Force Base, Tex.

Also helping with the administrative chores were William Kunisch, U.S. Army Recruiting Command, Fort Knox, Ky.; JOC Mike Marsh, Atlantic Fleet, Norfolk, Va.; Lt. Patrick Moore, Navy Chief of Information, Washington, D.C.; Capt. Mike Newman, Headquarters, U.S. Marine Corps; Capt. Dawson Plummer, Fort Knox, Ky.; Staff Sgt. Yvonne Reed, Marine Corps, Quantico, Va.; John Rickey, Fort Knox, Ky.; Lt. Mike Robinson, Navy Recruiting Command; Sgt. 1st Class James Rose, Army Training and Doctrine Command, Fort Monroe, Va.; Sgt. 1st Class David Rowell, Fort Knox, Ky.; Dave Smith, Air Force Training Command, Randolph Air Force Base, Tex.; Doug Smith, U.S. Army Recruiting Command, Fort Knox, Ky.; Maj. Bob Smith, U.S. Army Recruiting Command, Fort Knox, Ky.; Dean Sprague, Fort Knox, Ky.; Irma Thompson, Fort Benning,

Ga.; Dorothy Weir, MEPCOM, North Chicago, Ill.; and Lt. Rick Wester, Headquarters, U.S. Coast Guard.

Special thanks to some people who gave special support, including Vickie Lewis of The Lewis Group, Arlington, Va., for her graphics exper-tise; and Emily Birch of Greenwood Publishing Group for her support throughout the research and writing of this book.

✮ ✮ 1 ✮ ✮

WHO, ME? A SOLDIER?

In high school, I couldn't make up my mind whether to be a jock or a bookworm. Many things interested me, and I was even good at a few of them, especially basketball, debating and science. I could shoot hoops for hours or spend an entire afternoon sifting through books for a dynamite quote to use in the next debate tournament.

I could be a Nobel Prize winner, an NBA star, a top Hollywood actor, or even president of the United States. I was absolutely convinced of it. All I needed was to set my sights on a goal and start heading in that direction.

Oddly enough, that was part of the problem. When you choose to go down one path, you're also choosing not to go down dozens of other paths.

The question "What do you want to be when you grow up?" became tougher as I got older, even though I knew perfectly well what I wanted. I wanted to be an NBA star who spent some of the off-season in a science lab and some of it debating great ideas with the finest minds on the planet. Wasn't there a career somewhere that would let me do that?

The harder I thought about it, the farther I seemed to get from a decision. And the calendar was zipping along. Graduation day came closer and closer.

In the end, like more than 200,000 kids every year, I decided to take a time out—to go on a detour, to earn a little money, get a break from the books, and give myself time to sort out "the Big Career Question."

I decided to join the military.

WHAT I LEARNED ABOUT THE MILITARY

Probably the biggest surprise I had was that wearing a uniform didn't mean I was going to be yelled at all the time. Nor did it mean that I would be called put-down names or forced to do things that I thought were degrading.

High-ranking officers said please and thank you to me all the time. Senior people I worked with were genuinely friendly. They let me live my own life and do my job. On those occasions when I did something that probably deserved getting chewed out for, they'd most often take me aside, give me a chance to explain myself, and then tell me exactly where I had fallen short and what I needed to do to keep from getting in trouble again.

It was like getting straightened out by my favorite civilian boss.

Of course, everything wasn't roses and honey. I worked for one military guy I put near the top of my list of all-time, least favorite people. And there were times when people did, in fact, stand inches from my nose and raise their voices. Those real high-stress moments came at boot camp.

Boot camp is the first stop after coming on active duty. For about two months (exact periods vary by service; we'll go into that later), recruits are subject to round-the-clock training. They have absolutely no privacy and very little peace and quiet. They're constantly doing things that are physically demanding. Then there are those unforgettable moments when trainers decide to find out, in a very cold and deliberate way, how much pressure these new soldiers can stand.

Despite Hollywood horror stories about military training, I was never hit, never called an obscene name, and never singled out for ridicule. If I had to put one word on those first couple of months in uniform, that word would be "interesting." There was strange equipment to learn, rules of military life to master, and a thousand details to soak up, everything from the way to cross a field in combat to the difference between a major and a sergeant major.

"Is this what you're going to do for the rest of your life with a bunch of animals? Getting drunk every weekend?"

"No, after I graduate, I'm going to get drunk every night."

—Katy (Karen Allen) and Boon (Peter Riegert)
in *Animal House* (Universal Studios, 1978)

Perhaps one of the biggest surprises of all was that once boot camp was behind me, the rest of my time on active duty looked an awful lot like a regular job. I served my country in an office, and if you overlooked the uniforms, it was pretty much like any other office job. I had my own room off base. There were no morning physical fitness workouts or formal inspections.

Of course, friends who served in infantry units or aboard ship had more "military" in their daily lives. But even for them, day-to-day life in uniform had more similarities to than differences from civilian jobs.

Another big surprise didn't show up until my two-year hitch was over and I was looking for my first, real, postmilitary job. For some time, I had worried that I would lose ground next to friends who'd kept their noses to the grindstone in the civilian world. As it turned out, I never felt I had any catching up to do, because those two years in uniform hadn't been spent standing in a corner. I was learning things, doing things, sharpening skills, and proving my dependability. Most civilian bosses saw me as a good catch.

WHAT THE MILITARY MEANT TO ME

Those two years on active duty are very important to me—more important, frankly, than civilian jobs that lasted much longer.

Being in the armed forces was different from anything else I've ever done. I wasn't in combat, and my military duties didn't take me out of the country, but I still went places and did things most of my nonmilitary friends couldn't match.

The first man who hired me after my discharge gave a lot of weight to the fact that I was a veteran. I know, because we talked about it. He didn't have to worry whether I would show up at work on time, whether I could follow directions, or how I reacted under stress. I was a "good hire," even though my military duties had nothing to do with my civilian job.

Having been on active duty, I qualified for financial payments for education under a program known as the GI Bill. Although the word "scholarship" isn't used in connection with the GI Bill, that's how it operates. It's not a loan that must be repaid. It's a monthly check that was paid directly to me, to be used in whatever manner I wanted, so long as I was enrolled in school. The GI Bill made it possible for me to go to graduate school and earn a master's degree.

The military gave me something else that I hadn't seen much during my life—a savings account. By some standards, military pay is low. But some of that money isn't taxed, and there are other benefits, like free housing and free food, that have a definite and positive impact on the wallet. So like many veterans, I ended up leaving active duty with more money than I had when I started.

I also know (*Warning: syrupy moment approaching*) that I stepped forward and assumed the responsibilities of serving my country. Those aren't hollow words. I took on one of the most important responsibilities of citizenship, and I did all right. I paid my dues.

NOW FOR THE BAD NEWS

A debate has been going on in this country for longer than the United States has existed as a nation. Should every person have a legal obligation to serve in the military? Different answers have been given at different times in our history.

Since 1973, the answer has been no. Membership in the military has been voluntary since then. Although all eighteen-year-old males must register for the draft, there is no draft. Under current rules, you're not going to wear a uniform of the U.S. armed forces unless you volunteer.

Should you? If the military is such a good deal, shouldn't everybody? Again, the answer is no. Not everyone is cut out to be a soldier. Let's look at some specific people who should not be walking into a recruiter's office.

You Think the Military Is Just Another Job

The all-important fact, which no one should lose sight of, is that the U.S. armed forces exist to fight. Everything about them is focused upon combat. People running military pay offices, driving trucks, or cooking food must be prepared to do those jobs in a combat environment. The folks who keep airplanes in the sky, ships under way, and artillery batteries in readiness train at a demanding pace, even when no bad guy is out there on the international scene, threatening people and causing harm.

You don't have to be a chest-thumping, saber-rattling Rambo to be on active duty. In fact, since they're the ones who are put in harm's way when

Warning: The U.S. military is not just another employer
with a strict dress code.

the diplomats fail, military folks tend to be strong supporters of the peaceful resolution of the world's problems.

Religious and ethical convictions prevent some people from bearing arms, under any circumstances, against any foe. If you have those beliefs, if you can say that armed combat is always wrong, and you can't think of any circumstances in which it's right, then you shouldn't join the military.

You Have to Lie to Get In

It wasn't that long ago that some judges gave youthful offenders the choice of jail time or enlisting in the military. Those judges saw the military as a way to straighten out young people who were heading down a bad path.

Those days disappeared a while ago. Even though stories regularly appear in the news media about the military having recruiting problems, the folks already in uniform always put the people they accept through a careful screening. Serious criminal records and chronic drug problems are disqualifiers from military service.

If you have those kinds of problems in your past, it's better to level with the recruiter than to try hiding them. Your problems might fall in the category of youthful indiscretions that the armed forces may be willing to overlook. If the facts about your past surface after the military has invested serious money in your training, the consequences could be grim, with jail time and fines within the range of punishments.

You Think You Can Get Out Easily

The military is a volunteer force these days. Right? And "a volunteer" is someone who wants to be there. Right? And that means that if you enlist and don't like it, you can just walk away. Right?

Wrong! The military looks upon new recruits as investments. Before a new recruit leaves home for boot camp, that person already represents an investment to the military of tens of thousands of dollars. The investment snowballs rapidly once a recruit begins formal training.

To be in the military, people sign a formal, legally binding contract. The military promises certain training, assignments, or bonuses; the recruit promises to serve. The government doesn't make it easy for anyone to break that contract.

Just remember: Uniforms don't come with Velcro fasteners. They're not easy to take off.

You Don't Want to Be There

Spending a couple years of your life in a place you don't want to be doesn't make much sense at any age, for any reason. The military is a strange, demanding way of life that's tough even for people who are determined to fit in. It can be pure hell for those who don't want to be there.

If you're being led to the recruiting office by something other than your own wishes, better call a halt and take stock of what you really want. Being apprehensive before taking on a major commitment is perfectly normal; spending hours before you join thinking of ways to stay a civilian isn't.

Over the years, people have joined the military for a wide variety of reasons, from the perfectly solid to the totally flaky. What nudges you through the door isn't important. The decisive factor is the one between your two ears. What does the military offer that fits into the pattern you want for your own life?

Do you really want to be a soldier?

SPECIAL PEOPLE, SPECIAL CONSIDERATIONS

Joining one of the uniformed services is a major commitment for anyone. For some people, there are implications that don't affect the majority of new recruits. Let's look at a few of them.

You're Married

Today's military prides itself upon being family friendly. Most people in uniform are married, including a large percentage of those reporting for boot camp. Pentagon leaders (who have families of their own) know that the troops will be happiest and most productive when they can spend time regularly with their loved ones.

But the job comes first. Remember that the McDonald's restaurant chain exists to sell burgers, but the U.S. military exists to protect the nation. Guess who loses if the choice is between the nation's security and your chance to spend Christmas with the kids?

Don't count on seeing much of your family during the first six months on active duty. During that time, recruits learn the basic military skills upon which their usefulness to the armed forces depends. Families are distractions, and the military can—and will—make it impossible to see your family.

Again, that's during boot camp and individual training. Once new military members pass to their first assignments, many are heartened by the benefits available to spouses and kids.

For others, on-again–off-again problems of getting family time continue throughout their active-duty careers because they're in jobs that demand frequent assignments away from families. This is most likely to happen to soldiers and Marines in the infantry, sailors with shipboard skills, and airmen who maintain fighters and cargo planes.

You're a Single Parent

Many folks are surprised to learn that recruiters will take people who have children but not spouses. And recruiters shouldn't care whether or not someone was ever married. So long as they meet the standards—and the military has an opening they're qualified for—single parents can come put on a uniform. This applies to the active-duty force as well as the reserves and the National Guard. This is true for enlisted people and officers.

But if you're responsible for raising a child alone, you should be aware of a couple of facts before you walk into the recruiter's office. First, you will be separated from your child during boot camp and probably in the next stage of training, in which you learn a specific military skill.

That's going to happen, and there is no way around it. Sometimes the military comes first. The military insists upon having everyone's full attention during those first months on active duty.

The fact that no one can predict when another occasion will arise that demands your full attention to military duties leads to a second situation that single parents should know about before they begin talking to a recruiter. Single parents have to designate someone who will take care of the kids if they are suddenly called away.

That plan has to be in writing and filed with the unit commander. It has to be specific enough so that someone else can take that piece of paper and make the arrangements if the parent is unable to get to a phone. The plan will be reviewed every year by the unit commander.

Can you leave your child in the care of others for your first six months on active duty? Can you put your child in someone else's care and march away into a combat zone? If the answer to either of these questions is no, then you shouldn't even start on the path that leads to the recruiter's office.

You're a Woman

Since the early 1970s, women have been moving into more military jobs. Now they can pilot combat aircraft and serve aboard most ships. Still closed are the combat-related jobs on the ground—infantry, artillery, and armor—where physical strength and a lack of privacy are concerns.

Official policy is that women are treated like men. They're paid the same, given the same assignments and promotions, subjected in the same ways to career opportunities and hazardous duty.

The flip side of that is that military women don't get many special breaks. Women with children, even if they're single parents, must do their jobs, including jobs that send them into combat zones.

Pregnancy used to be an automatic reason for discharge. Now, it's the other way around; the rules are written to keep pregnant women on active duty. Getting out requires a struggle, even for single parents.

Sexual harassment pops into the headlines from time to time, and there's no denying that it exists in the military, just as it does in the rest of society. There's no evidence that it's worse in the military. In fact, all sorts of antiharassment orders are on the books, and unit commanders know their careers are over if they bungle an investigation into these charges.

Some bad feelings still exist toward women, often with a kernel of reason. Folks in ground-combat units and on sea duty may see military women as making their jobs harder. The thinking is that for every woman in uniform who can't serve in a ground-combat or shipboard assignment, a male is likely to have to spend more time from his family.

You're in a Minority

More than any other segment of society, the military has worked to make itself color blind. And it has largely succeeded. The color of your skin, the language you were taught as a child, the place you were born, the name you use for your God—none should have any bearing upon your treatment in the military.

Few civilian employers have African-Americans and Hispanics in such numbers throughout the supervisory levels, middle management, and even upper management.

As with the larger society, the armed forces cannot provide a guarantee that you won't run across someone who is narrow minded and intolerant. But the large number of minority members spread throughout the military's rank structure, plus formal programs to protect the interests of minorities, makes the military pretty inhospitable for bigots.

But be warned: The military works without what's come to be known as "affirmative action." It offers no special deals to anyone because of heritage. Instead, Pentagon leaders strive to ensure that everyone is treated with strict equality in the basics—same pay, same housing, same rules of personal behavior.

———————— ☆ ————————

"It's a term of service, not a career. I just want to get out on my own.
See the galaxy for a couple years."

—Johnny Rico (Casper Van Dien) in *Starship Troopers*
(Columbia Pictures, 1997)

That also means that everyone gets the same training, where everyone is evaluated by the same standards. Those who rise fastest up the promotion ladder are those with the highest scores. Period.

You're Gay or Lesbian

One of the toughest segments of military life to see clearly involves gays and lesbians in uniform. Since the early 1990s, they have had a measure of protection from prosecution in the so-called "don't ask, don't tell" policy. Military commanders cannot delve into one of their subordinate's private sexual life out of idle curiosity. Recently, the military has strengthened protections for gays and lesbians, and increased the penalties for people who harass them.

How fairly have gays and lesbians been treated? It's almost impossible to get a realistic understanding. The gay community itself hasn't always been helpful, because it has a vested interest in hyping problems.

If truth be told (*Warning: one man's opinion coming*), two secrets underlie the military and its gays and lesbians, which neither side wants to advertise.

First, not only have gays and lesbians always been a part of military life, but most have served with no problems. They've kept their private lives private, and the vast majority of commanders—even the ones who know the truth—are interested in judging them strictly on the basis of their job performance. The days being hounded by the military for visiting a gay bar seem to be over.

Second, a certain proportion of the gays and lesbians who run afoul of the military have asked for trouble. They brought their private lives into their units. They acted in ways that, had they been heterosexual, would have still created problems.

What's the worst that can happen? For those whose orientation, for whatever reason, fair or unfair, becomes an issue of official military interest, the worst that usually happens is that they're discharged. They're not court-martialed, not imprisoned, not fined, not given a dishonorable discharge. They're shown the door.

Tougher treatment is in store for anyone whom commanders believe is making unwanted advances toward another member of the unit. Count on being handled in the same way as a heterosexual who made the wrong moves on an unwilling partner.

★ ★ 2 ★ ★

A SNAPSHOT OF YOU
IN UNIFORM

Have you caught yourself daydreaming about what it would be like to be in the military? Where would they send you? What would you do all day? What if there were a war?

Chapters later in this book have the answers to many questions that are in the minds of would-be recruits, along with some that people typically don't start thinking of until they're packing for boot camp.

High school students who see the military as one option in a wide array of choices they can make aren't interested in the difference between the Basic Allowance for Housing and the Overseas Housing Allowance. They want the Big Picture, the Bottom Line, the Down and Dirty. So, let's get to it.

A COMPLETE MILITARY CAREER IN TEN EASY STEPS

Everyone who enlists in the military goes through the same basic ten steps. That's true whether they stay two years on active duty or twenty.

(Officers are in a different situation. As you'll see in later chapters, there are many different routes to becoming an officer. Once they're in uniform, however, they follow the same basic path as enlisted folks.)

Here are the basic steps followed by everyone who joins the military as an enlisted member.

Step One: The Recruiter

The military has people in every community whose job is to bring folks onto active duty. They're called recruiters.

A recruiter will weed out those who clearly don't qualify. The recruiter will answer questions, explain how things work, and help people with paperwork.

A recruiter can offer some incentives. Those incentives include the job for which the military will train a person, the place he or she will be assigned after training, when a person would come on active duty, and—within a narrow range—the rank.

Some people receive lump-sum payments, called "enlistment bonuses." These payments are made to people who sign up for specific skills. Most skills don't come with enlistment bonuses. For those that do, payment of the bonus is automatic.

Everyone coming into the military agrees to serve for a specific length of time, usually between two and six years.

Step Two: MEPS

If the recruiter thinks a would-be soldier is qualified to join the service and the would-be soldier still wants to serve, the next step is the Military Entrance Processing Station, or MEPS (rhymes with "steps").

MEPS is the place where the military gives physicals to people before they join. These facilities are within a day's bus ride of most communities.

A trip to the local MEPS facility is usually scheduled weeks in advance. People arrive late in the evening, they're given rooms at government expense in a local motel, and they start the physicals early the next morning.

Two other steps take place at the MEPS center before would-be recruits get back on the bus and head home.

Step Three: Aptitude Tests

You might want a certain military job. You may even have practical experience or have taken classes that show you know how to do that job. But the armed forces won't give it to you until you've passed tests that prove to them that you've got what it takes.

———— ⭐ ————

"Listen, Centauri, I'm a kid from a trailer park."

"If that's what you think, then that's all you'll ever be."

—Alex (Lance Guest) and Centauri (Robert Preston)
in *The Last Starfighter* (Universal Studios, 1984)

The tests are called the Armed Services Vocational Aptitude Battery, ASVAB (pronounced "AS-vab"). Usually, they're administered at the MEPS center after the physical exams.

Step Four: Taking the Oath

There is a clear, legal dividing line between a civilian and a soldier. It comes when people raise their hands and take an oath. At that moment, even though they've never put on a uniform, they are legally members of the U.S. military, entitled to the military pay and benefits, and subject to military discipline.

Generally, the oath is administered at the MEPS center. Recruits also sign a form, an enlistment contract, that spells out exactly what they've been promised if they come on active duty and the length of time they've agreed to serve.

Step Five: Boot Camp

Everyone goes through the same intensive training course to learn the basics about the military—how to salute, how to wear the uniform, how to fire a weapon and operate as a member of a unit. And there's physical conditioning, lots and lots of physical conditioning.

This training base has a variety of official names. Most people know it simply as "boot camp."

Each service runs its own boot camp. Depending on the service, boot camp lasts from nine to thirteen weeks. If you can't complete boot camp, you can't go into the military.

Although Hollywood likes to depict boot camp as a place where people are physically and psychologically abused, it's not like that. Yes, it's deliberately stressful. But more than 200,000 people go through it every year. You can do it.

When a recruit goes to boot camp is something that's worked out with a recruiter. There are no surprises. Some people choose to go directly from the MEPS center, others wait for up to a year after the MEPS screening.

Step Six: Individual Training

Boot camp gives people the basic information they need to be soldiers, sailors, airmen, Marines, or Coast Guardsmen. But that's not enough to make folks useful members of the military. They also need a skill.

After boot camp, every member of the Army, Air Force, and Marine Corps will go to another training course where they will learn about a specific military skill. There are no surprises here. Before new recruits take the enlistment oath, they will learn from their recruiter exactly which course they will attend, how long it lasts, and where it's located.

The duration of these courses depends upon the skill. They can last a couple of weeks, a couple of months, or even longer. Some of these skill-producing training courses are at the same location as the boot camp, but others are at other installations.

New members of the Navy and Coast Guard may also go to a school after boot camp to learn a skill, or they may go directly from boot camp to their first assignment. For them, the military skill will come through a combination of on-the-job training and correspondence courses. Again, there are no surprises. New sailors and Coasties will know before they come on active duty how their skill training will be handled.

Step Seven: First Assignment

After new recruits go through boot camp and training in their military skill, they're sent to their first assignment.

But they are still learning the ropes, so the newest members of the military usually find constant reminders that they're not working for Burger King. They will probably have to live on a military installation, perhaps even in some sort of dormitory. They will have to inform their commanders if they want to see a doctor or take a couple of days off.

Someone coming on active duty for two years may only have one assignment. Longer periods in uniform are practically guaranteed to be involved if you get more than one assignment.

Before you start on active duty, your recruiter might be able to tell you where your first assignment will be. The recruiter may even been able to guarantee it.

Step Eight: The Rest of Your (Military) Life

Whether you stay two years in uniform or twenty, you'll find yourself subject to many of the same patterns.

- At regular intervals, usually between every two years and four years, you'll be reassigned. The military will ask where you'd like to go, but you'll move where—and when—the military orders you.
- Every few years, you'll have the chance to earn promotions. Early in your career, the promotions will be nearly automatic. As you advance, they'll become more competitive and less predictable.

- You'll never stop studying. At least once every five years, the military will send you to a full-time school to brush up on your skills. The rewards for doing well include the quickest promotions and the best assignments.
- You will be expected to stay in good physical condition, although the exact standards will ease the older you get.
- Living in a goldfish bowl—that's one description of life in uniform. Problems that civilian bosses don't notice, like indebtedness, can end careers. If you work in a field that requires a security clearance, your personal life will have to be almost spotless.

Step Nine: Leaving

The foundation of your relationship with the military is the contract you signed at the recruiters'. One of the key elements of that enlistment contract is the period you agreed to serve on active duty.

Once that period is over, you're free to go home. If you choose to stay a little longer in uniform (and if the military wants you), you'll sign another contract that commits you to another number of years.

Generally, leaving before your obligation is over isn't an option. It does, however, happen. Reasons for an early release include:

- A physical problem prevents you from serving.
- A family hardship justifies a compassionate discharge.
- The military releases you because it's not happy with your performance.
- The military releases you because it has too many people with your skill and rank.
- You're qualified for a full-time degree-producing program, which requires you to come back to the military after graduation.

Most of these rules apply equally to enlisted people and to officers.

There is one major difference. Although officers are obligated to serve a certain number of years—anywhere from two to eight—when they first

———— ☆ ————

"You learn to think in terms of the group, you learn to remember,
you learn to think of your responsibilities and you learn
to carry out orders."

—Tech.Sgt. Jim Moore (Jack Webb) in *The DI*
(Warner Brothers, 1957)

come on active duty, they don't formally commit themselves to serving for a specific number of years after that initial obligation is met. They can resign at any time.

Everyone leaving the military receives a form, called discharge papers, or DD Form 214, that shows they've served on active duty, lists their medals, and records some other information.

Those discharge papers also record whether you did a good job (which leads to what the military calls an "honorable discharge"), an okay job (a "general discharge") or a bad job (a "dishonorable discharge"). Many veterans programs hinge upon getting an honorable or a general discharge. A dishonorable discharge bars former service members from most of the benefits the government offers to veterans.

Everyone leaving the military knows about it months in advance. The government picks up the costs of getting recently discharged military people back home. That includes their personal property.

Step Ten: A Veteran

Taking off the uniform doesn't end your connection with the military. A kinship unites everyone who has served in the armed forces.

Even in this cynical age, you will be recognized as a member of a special group, a breed apart. For the rest of your life, you will be called a veteran.

(*Warning: Another syrupy moment*) You can stand shoulder to shoulder with men and women who have served this country during wars and during times of peace. You may be eligible to join organizations like the Veterans of Foreign Wars (VFW) and the American Legion. Even if you don't join any group, you'll carry a certain responsibility—and authority—when its comes to instructing younger generations in the lessons of citizenship.

Some future Veterans Day, even if you stand quietly amid the crowd on the sidewalk, you'll realize that all the music, hoopla, and marching is for you.

THE DOLLARS AND CENTS OF PATRIOTISM

Today's military doesn't expect sheer patriotism to propel people into the recruiting office. Since the early 1970s, the United States has had an all-volunteer force, and a wide array of benefits are available to make service financially attractive.

We will go into many of these benefits in greater detail later, but, since we're only interested in putting together a snapshot of military life, let's focus on the major benefits.

Pay

In the year 2000, every recruit starts out with at least $930 per month. That increases in four months to at least $1,005. By the time of the first anniversary of enlisting, the majority of new service members were earning at least $1,127.

That money has a bigger wallop than you'd expect. For during boot camp and skill-related training—a period of four to six months—the military provides three meals a day and a place to live, without deducting anything from pay.

Travel

The military will pay to get you to boot camp. It will pick up the bill to get you to anywhere you're officially assigned. The travel pay includes money for food. That doesn't mean you can book your own flights and expect reimbursements for fancy meals. It means that generally the government will make the arrangements, which will be okay, not deluxe.

Sickness

The military gives free medical care to everyone on active duty. Members of the armed forces draw full pay while ill. If new recruits miss too much training due to illness, they may find themselves ordered to repeat the course, even boot camp.

Time Off

Everyone on active duty gets thirty days' paid vacation every year. It's called "leave." Don't count on getting any leave during boot camp, and don't expect much during the next step in your training, where you learn a skill. Exceptions are made for genuine family emergencies. But, as with missing time due to illnesses, even an officially approved leave of absence can send you back to the beginning of a course.

—————— ☆ ——————

"A gladiator is like a stallion. He must be pampered."

—Batiatus (Peter Ustinov) in *Spartacus*
(Universal Studios, 1960)

Shopping

Most military installations have stores that sell most items of daily life at reduced rates. "Commissaries" are the military's food stores, and "exchanges" are department stores.

Entertainment

Other on-base facilities typically range from swimming pools and movie theaters to bowling alleys and shops for the do-it-yourself auto mechanic. Most of these facilities are free, although things like theaters and bowling alleys may charge fees, which are quite small next to the off-base competition.

Families

Spouses and children don't live with new recruits at boot camp, but they are eligible for free or reduced-rate medical care and access to on-base stores and entertainment facilities. The service member also receives extra pay to cover housing costs for the family.

Education

Military training is free, and the armed forces encourage everyone in uniform to take college-level courses. If the military sees a connection between a civilian course and your military duties, the government will pick up 75 percent of the cost. The program that offers that is called "tuition assistance."

The more commonly known Montgomery GI Bill offers money to pay educational bills for college-level courses and many vocational classes, whether or not they are job-related. Although the Montgomery GI Bill is commonly associated with veterans, people on active duty can use it to help pay their educational bills, too.

Disability Coverage

If something makes you physically unable to continue in uniform, you'll be discharged. The Department of Veterans Affairs (the VA) will provide free lifetime medical care for that condition and a tax-free monthly payment ranging from about $100 to about $2,000 (year 2000 rates) monthly, depending on the severity of the problem.

2777058

Life Insurance

Everyone on active duty can purchase up to $200,000 in life insurance for eighteen dollars a month. Nothing in the civilian world comes close to that. Plan on taking it.

AND NOW, THE DOWNSIDE

Admittedly, this depiction of the military has been upbeat. We've been trying to present a snapshot of what you'd look like in uniform, and nobody wants their photograph taken next to an overflowing garbage pail. What about the downside?

The most powerful reasons to stay out of uniform are highly personal. Is a parent in poor health? Do you have an opportunity to go to college that might not be there in a few years? Can you make substantially more money than the military has to offer? Or, as we've talked about earlier, is your enlisting somebody else's idea, that you don't like?

Let's look at a few other issues:

It's Not a Job, It's a Commitment

Everyone's relationship with the military is based upon a legally binding contract. You can't walk away if you think it was a bad decision. Desertion is a crime, and people wind up in jail every day because they tried to walk away from Uncle Sam before they fulfilled their enlistment contracts.

The First Couple of Months Are Tough

Most Hollywood depictions of boot camp are wrong. It's not a place where people are hit by drill instructors and called horrible names. In some respects it's worse: boot camp includes some carefully calculated moments of extreme pressure during which both you and the military get a rough idea how you'd perform in combat.

You're Not Running Your Own Life

The toughest thing about the military for many people—including those who loved their time in uniform—is the fact that someone else makes many of the major decisions affecting their lives. Where you live, whether you can take an after-hours second job, whether you can sign up for classes, sometimes even the people you can socialize with—these are among life's small decisions that can be taken out of your hands once you enlist.

Your Family Is in It, Too

Once you put on the uniform, the long arm of Uncle Sam also reaches to your family. Your commander can't prohibit your family from joining you overseas, but the military can refuse to pay their travel expenses and deny them on-base housing. Sometimes—and boot camp is a prime example—commanders can restrict people to stay on base in areas closed to civilians, thus making it impossible even to talk to loved ones.

★ ★ 3 ★ ★

MILITARY LIFE

About 1.6 million people serve on active duty in the military. Ask what it's like or why they joined or what they expect from the service and you'll get 1.6 million different answers.

But if you talk to enough people, some common threads will emerge. Earning educational benefits, seeing the world, being on your own, taking a break from the books—these are at the top of most lists. In truth, most people don't join for a single reason. A variety of factors, each carrying a different importance, are jumbled together to motivate each individual.

You're the only one who can sort through your own reasons and decide whether they're sufficient to take on the responsibilities of joining the military. Is the military right for you? Only you can say.

But instead of giving you more facts and figures, let's look at the experiences of six typical people who looked at their options after high school and decided to spend at least a few years in uniform.

SUSAN'S STORY: ONE EXPLOSIVE DAY AFTER ANOTHER

When a strange package without a return address appeared outside the door of a general's home, they called for Susan Nichols.

Nichols, a slim brunette from Denver, is willing to step into situations when the toughest warriors often back away.

She is learning the skills of an explosive ordnance disposal (EOD) expert in the Air Force. Taking unexploded weapons—from missiles and bombs to biological weapons, unidentified packages and pipe bombs—and making them safe to be around is what she does for a living.

"My grandmother told everybody what I was going to do as soon as I enlisted," said Nichols, now twenty-one and wearing the three stripes of a senior airman. "The reactions of people went from, You must be crazy, to, That's cool."

Nichols sees her job as neither crazy nor cool. To listen to her, it's also one of the safest jobs in the military.

"We do things as safely as possible. If it's possible, we're going to send in a robot. We're going to take as many precautions as we can."

Sadly, she's in a growth industry. Some terrorist groups see the U.S. military as the enemy. The bomb squad is called to look at packages that a few years ago would have been opened and inspected by anyone curious about their contents.

Nichols is learning to identify and deal with biological and chemical hazards. And there are things that aren't bombs but pack a tremendous wallop. The ejection seats and canopies of modern jets rely on explosives to work. They fall under Nichols's range of professional interests.

One thing she hasn't been involved with is a scene that's become a Hollywood cliché. In countless movies, the fearless bomb-squad member is trying to defuse an explosive that is ticking down to a demolition. It comes down to two wires. Cutting one will make the bomb harmless, cutting the other will set it off.

"If it comes down to a red wire and a green wire and you're guessing what to do, that's pretty bad."

Six and a half months of specialized training were necessary after boot camp for Nichols to become qualified as an explosive ordnance disposal apprentice. She receives $150 monthly in hazardous duty pay in addition to her regular pay.

Sometimes, she's on call twenty-four hours a day. Also, whereas most airmen don't take daily physical training after boot camp, the EOD folks must work out three times a week.

---- ★ ----

"If everywhere in the world were like home,
there'd be no reason to leave."

—Clark Griswald (Chevy Chase) in
National Lampoon's Vacation
(Warner Brothers, 1983)

Nichols chose this unconventional field after carefully balancing a variety of factors.

"I didn't want to do something in the military that felt like I wasn't in the military," she said. She also wanted something that was outdoors and less book oriented, even though she plans to pick up her college education where she left it before enlisting, in the middle of her sophomore year.

While she works in a predominately male career field, Nichols said gender hasn't been an issue. "You want to get along. Men should feel comfortable [around active-duty women]. They shouldn't have to worry about saying the wrong thing. But there's also this line that can't be crossed."

Although she's single, she said she doesn't feel that men are put off when they find out that she blows things up for a living.

The daughter of a career Air Force enlisted man, Nichols said she hasn't decided whether or not she'll make a career of the military. That depends upon her job prospects in a few years after she earns her bachelor's degree.

So far, all her emergency calls have been harmless—like the suspicious package on the general's doorstep. It was a fruitcake.

MARK'S STORY: ON A WELL-TRAVELED ROAD TO SUCCESS

Mark Wakefield didn't need a recruiting poster to join the military. All he needed was to look around his hometown.

Many of the men he admired—like a history teacher and the assistant manager at a local supermarket—were veterans.

"The Army taught them about leadership and team work. It made them successful because they knew how to make employees work with them."

Growing up in foster homes, Mark appreciated people who could walk into any situation and know how to deal with strangers. He began to notice those traits while serving in the junior ROTC program in high school in West Valley, Utah.

After graduation, he went into pre-med studies at a local college, but by the time of the Christmas break of his freshman year Mark began to have serious discussions with military recruiters.

Like many people who join the military, Mark can't point to a single reason for doing it. The feeling that he needed some maturity before continuing with college, the desire to earn GI Bill educational benefits, the sense that enlisting was a way of paying a debt to this country, the adventure of a new way of life—all of these reasons and more came into play.

His first conversations were with Marine Corps recruiters. He ended up enlisting in the Army, because Army recruiters were willing to give him more options.

He chose the infantry ("If you're going to join the Army, why not get the full experience?") and passed up a recruiting bonus of $12,000 to get special additions to the basic GI Bill benefits that ended up being worth $40,000.

Mark has already done the math. When he gets out after his four-year hitch, he'll have $1,111.11 per month to spend on education and living expenses for a typical nine-month school year.

But that's in the future. He has gone through boot camp, then three more weeks of grueling physical training to become "airborne," which is what the Army calls its parachute troops. He plans to attend the Army's ranger school. That's a course that can make the toughest boot camp look like a Sunday picnic.

"I want the biggest challenges I can get. I want it to be as hard as it can be, so that I know it will only make me tougher."

These days, he works in the office of a training unit at Fort Benning, Ga., one of the Army's largest training installations. Although he's been in uniform only about a year, he is a private and has his own room with a microwave and shower.

A host of things to do when he's not on duty—from movie theaters and clubs to hobby shops and college courses—are within walking distance. Prices for everything are lower than they are off base.

Being an infantryman means that he's a candidate to be sent into any international hot spot that gets out of control. "I think about it, but it doesn't scare me," Mark says. "I'm confident in the training I've received."

GEORGE'S STORY: FINDING A VILLAGE UNDER THE WAVES

George Benecke's bed is a mattress between two torpedoes. His "closet" is an empty space at the foot of the mattress mostly taken up with the books he must study to earn promotion as a sonar technician.

There's no room for the guitar that he used to play in bands growing up in Brooklyn.

Benecke's life changed a few years ago when he answered the telephone at home. It was the wrong number, but Benecke found himself talking to the man on the other end of the line. It was a military recruiter.

"There was nothing for me out there in the world," he said. "I was a screw-up in high school, on my own pretty young."

He had toyed with the idea of following his father, a wounded Vietnam veteran, into the Marine Corps, but the recruiter on the other end of the line that fateful day was a Navy recruiter.

———— ★ ————

"I've died and gone to Gomer Pyle's house."

—Teacher Bill Rago (Danny DeVito) in
Renaissance Man (Touchstone Pictures, 1994)

So it was into the Navy that Benecke went.

"People shouldn't be intimidated about going into the military because of boot camp. It's a short time," he said. "But if you're not willing to put 100 percent into it, you won't get much out of it."

Benecke was attracted to the world of submarines. It's an elite force within the Navy. Everyone is a volunteer. With about 120 people on a boat—submarines are "boats," not "ships"—you know the people you serve with. You also know many of their jobs.

After boot camp, he spent six weeks attending the Navy's basic enlisted submarine course, then another sixteen weeks learning the basics of being a sonarman.

Two days after reporting for duty aboard the USS *Oklahoma City*, he was at sea.

The *Oklahoma City* is a nuclear-powered attack sub. Traditionally, its job has been to attack enemy submarines and surface vessels. Now it also carries cruise missiles, which permit it to attack land targets.

The passageways—as hallways are called aboard ship—are so narrow that people coming from opposite ends must flatten themselves against a wall to pass.

Sleeping on a mattress in the torpedo room is something of a luxury in the submarine force. On some vessels, two men on different shifts are assigned to the same bed. It's called "hot racking."

Still, Benecke has no intention of applying for a job in a part of the Navy that sees more sunlight.

"It's more like an elite club," he says. "Down here, you know everybody, and you have more opportunities to learn about different jobs."

JOSE'S STORY: JUST TRY TICKETING A MARINE

Jose Zepeda was a cop in Roswell, New Mexico, when he pulled over a car for speeding and his life changed.

"I went to give this guy a ticket. I saw he had on his Marine Corps dress blues [the Corps' fanciest uniform]. I couldn't give him a ticket."

Of course, there was a buildup to that life-changing moment: like Jose's respect for his dad, who was wounded as a Marine in combat in Vietnam; like the tough road Jose had traveled after high school.

The youngest of eleven children, he had worked full time on the police force, trying to find the time for college courses. Education was the key to advancement in any field.

Jose knew about the Montgomery GI Bill, America's "thank you" to its veterans, which provided money for education to those who serve in uniform, plus the various programs that help people still on active duty get degrees.

It all came together when Jose stopped that Marine, who was, no doubt, on his way to a party or some ceremony.

But Jose faced a problem that is common to people who first talk to the recruiter a few years after graduation. He had already started working his way up the ladder. Enlisting would cut his income in half. But a few sacrifices now would put Jose far ahead in the future.

His recruiter was an ally, a professional who knew the ropes and wanted him to be prepared. His drill sergeant was another story, tougher, more demanding, unpleasant, although Jose says he wouldn't hesitate to go through boot camp again.

"There were days I was thinking that I wouldn't give them the satisfaction of failing. But, looking back, I can see I wouldn't have made it without my drill instructors. I was out of shape, and they motivated me."

With six years of solid civilian experience as a cop, he was a natural to become an MP, as the Marines call a military policeman.

But being a natural fit for a military job doesn't always mean you get it. Sometimes, there are more practical problems—like discovering that all the seats in the next MP training course were already taken.

Jose slid smoothly into a related field. He was selected for training in intelligence, but suddenly another complication arose. For some time, he had relied on credit cards to get him through a number of financial crises, including the drop in his living that came with his enlistment. He was thousands of dollars in debt.

---------- ✯ ----------

"Greetings, starfighter. You have been recruited by the Star League to defend the frontier against Xur and the Ko-Dan armada."

—Centauri (Robert Preston) in *The Last Starfighter* (Universal Studios, 1984)

In the civilian world, a worker in debt is someone with a personal problem. But in the military, things are different. Troops with financial troubles can be ordered into financial counseling or they're seen as security risks. Jose was told his debts would keep him out of intelligence work.

Fortunately, Jose's problems weren't enough to get him discharged from active duty. He was reclassified as an emergency medical technician, given financial counseling, and sent off to learn his new skill.

In four years on active duty, Jose has managed to get out of debt, work his way up to corporal, earn an associate's degree, get married, and start a family.

"I may think about staying in the Marines if I can become a cop again," he said.

Only this time, any speeders he pulls over aren't likely to escape without a ticket because they have a uniform.

MATTHEW'S STORY: STAYING HOME BY GOING AWAY

For centuries, people have gone to sea to run away, to get a taste of a different life. Matthew Flynn went to sea to get closer to home.

Matthew grew up along the Maryland shore. Crabbing and boating were as much a part of his life as baseball and homework. His proudest possession is a seventeen-foot, ninety-horsepower Boston whaler.

Like many people joining the military, Matthew saw education as a major incentive. He planned to spend a few years in uniform, earn some money, and get Montgomery GI Bill benefits for college.

"It didn't take the recruiter any work to get me to sign up."

But Matthew had some priorities in his life that he couldn't ignore, some obligations, and people who were important to him—like a fiancé and parents he wanted to stay close to.

A Coast Guard recruiter was willing to guarantee Matthew an assignment close to home. That service has many small facilities—called "stations," often with only a couple of dozen people—dotting the coastline.

So, instead of joining the Navy, where crews aboard aircraft carriers can number in the thousands and it's possible to spend days afloat without emerging to look at a wave, Matthew chose the branch of the military that in peacetime is run by the Transportation Department, not the Pentagon, where the vessels and the bases tend to be smaller.

That doesn't mean that Coast Guard boot camp is any less demanding that those run by the other services. In fact, Matthew's recruiter persuaded him to begin running and working out before he reported for training. The recruiter also convinced him to quit smoking.

None of the services permit recruits to smoke. That includes lighting up after hours or off base. None. Zero. Zip.

That was one of the better pieces of boot camp advice that Matthew received. "It would have been really rough if, on top of everything else getting thrown at me, I had to deal with tobacco, too."

Boot camp for Coast Guardsmen—or "Coasties"—is similar to the basic training courses run by the other services: physical conditioning, classes, practical exercises, long hours, drill instructors who aren't shy about raising their voices.

Sit-ups had always been Matthew's weak point. In fact, up until the final exam he hadn't been able to make the minimum number of sit-ups. If he failed—which seemed likely—he'd have to repeat at least a week of boot camp.

"During the final test, I had the instructors and the company commander yelling at me, getting me to keep going. I finally made it. Afterward, they shook my hand. They're there to help you."

Since graduating from boot camp, Matthew, now a seaman apprentice, has been assigned to a small, thirty-person Coast Guard station on Maryland's shore of the Chesapeake Bay.

He shares a barracks room with another Coastie. He's on duty for forty-eight hours, then off for forty-eight.

Soon after reporting for duty, Matthew was standing watch, which involves monitoring the radio and dealing with calls from boaters in distress. "It can be very quiet, then it all comes at once. You get calls for four or five boats in a row. You've got to keep track of them and the boats that are going to help them and you've got to be calm. You're the one they're listening to."

Once he gets past his first year in uniform, Matthew plans to enroll in some college courses. His goal is to work in a branch of law enforcement where you're not likely to get your feet wet—specifically, the FBI.

Meanwhile, Matthew is doing what he likes in a place he enjoys being. "I love being on the water and helping people out," he said.

$\star\,\star\,4\,\star\,\star$

THE RECRUITER

If anyone wants to join the military—or if someone is just interested in exploring the possibility of joining—the place to go is to the office of the local military recruiter.

Recruiters are full-time professionals. Bringing people into the military is what they do for a living. They are trained to have the answers about military service that young people want to know. Because they're in the military themselves, recruiters can draw upon their experiences to help people understand what happens at boot camp and throughout a typical tour of duty.

Recruiters are the subject of a lot of misinformation. Hollywood loves to portray them as people who will say anything to get folks to put on a uniform. Some veterans will blame recruiters for not telling them about things that no one could possibly know.

Reality Check: Recruiters are human beings. As in any group of people, there are a few "bad apples" who distort things. But most are honest. They want the government to get high-quality recruits, and they want recruits to begin their time in uniform feeling good about the military. That doesn't happen if people feel they've been lied to or tricked into enlisting.

Perhaps the best way to begin understanding recruiters is to take a look at one.

KEITH'S STORY: LOOKING FOR GOLD

Keith Adams grew up in the shadow of the nation's capital. The White House was a few minutes' walk away. But, for him, Washington, D.C., was still an inner city, where opportunities were few and life could be tough.

"We had our problems, back when I was a kid, but it wasn't like today. We had our skirmishes, but we could solve them without gunfire."

As his high school graduation day approached, Adams took stock of his situation. Staying where he was wasn't an option, for that risked getting drawn into the life of the streets. College was in his plans, but he couldn't face four more years of hitting the books.

That's when he decided to have a chat with a military recruiter. "He was a laid-back guy, who didn't have to do much for me. Some of my buddies had just joined, and they filled me in on what to do. The recruiter did my paperwork, and the next time I saw him, I was getting on a train to go to boot camp."

It was just a break from the books and the chance to earn GI Bill benefits to pay for college. That much of Adams's story, at least, is typical.

But Adams went on to spend twenty years in uniform. One of his last assignments before retiring from the Marine Corps was a three-year hitch as a recruiter in Alexandria, Virginia, in the suburbs of his old hometown.

Recruiters are characters in a lot of movies. Almost always they're fast-talking hucksters who'll say anything to get someone to enlist.

But Hollywood has never done a good job capturing the one truth that is at the heart of all military recruiters: How well they do their job is seen on the battlefield. The young man or woman a recruiter helps sign up today may some day serve alongside the recruiter in some future firefight.

"First and foremost, we want to make sure that they can take up the challenge," Adams said. "The military is all about intangibles. If someone can't understand that, they're wasting their time coming to see a recruiter."

Adams, who is married and has four children ranging in age from fifteen to seven, puts in a seven-day week. For those long hours, he is paid an extra $375 a month.

Adams is credited with signing up more than seventy recruits during his three-years on the job, which is slightly above average for recruiters. The young people he remembers are the recruits whose life turned around abruptly when they joined the military.

"A lot of minimum-wage people don't think they're qualified. I'm talking all the time to the people who work in fast-food joints. In the movie theater, I'll end up talking to the person who gives me popcorn," Adams said.

"We're prospecting all the time." Adams added an interesting choice of words. He doesn't "look" for recruits. He "prospects." That's the word that miners use to describe their search for gold.

WORKING WITH A RECRUITER

Most communities have military recruiters. In rural areas, they're found in the county seat or the largest town in the area. The military likes to put them in the places people are, like shopping centers and downtown business districts.

In many communities, military recruiters share office space with each other. But that's purely for convenience. Each branch of the military has its own recruiters. An Army recruiter cannot help anyone join the Air Force, although much of the basic information that an Army recruiter has about military life—from pay rates and medical coverage to GI Bill benefits and veterans' programs—applies to people who join any branch of the armed forces.

Recruiters specialize in other ways. The military is divided into two groups of people—officers and enlisted folks. Officers are almost always college graduates; they have their own training courses; they also have their own recruiters. A typical military recruiter brings people into uniform with an enlisted rank. That typical recruiter can answer questions about becoming an officer, but the recruiter will usually refer qualified people to a specialized recruiter for help becoming an officer. (Chapter 5 looks at ways to become an officer.)

Another specialty among recruiters involves the division between active-duty and part-time military people. Active duty is full-time service in uniform. Reservists and National Guardsmen are people who hold civilian jobs but who take part in military training for one weekend a month and two weeks each summer. Although most reservists and guardsmen have already served on active duty, it's possible to become a reservist or National Guardsman directly from the civilian world.

As with officers, the typical recruiter can answer general questions about these part-time warriors. But people interested in becoming a reservist or Guardsman may discover that the local military recruiter will refer them to

--------- ★ ---------

Recruit: "What are these?—yachts?"

Recruiter: "The Army's the best kept secret in the world."

—Recruiter Sgt. Jim Ballard (Harry Dean Stanton) and
Judy Benjamin (Goldie Hawn) in *Private Benjamin*
(Warner Brothers, 1980)

someone else, probably outside the community. (Chapter 5 examines the direct route into the reserves and National Guard.)

Recruiters do more than help people fill out forms and answer questions. They're the first step in the military's intensive screening process. They want to make sure that potential recruits meet the minimum standards for military service. And they are also the first step in screening people to determine the military job that would best use their skills and interests.

The military expects them to do more than just send healthy young people to boot camp. They're also expected to keep a steady flow of qualified, motivated people heading into the thousands of training courses operated by the U.S. military. Recruiters know which training courses have vacancies and when they occur. A big part of the job of recruiters is to steer potential recruits into those courses that have vacancies. And, if the recruiters know that a certain course won't have a vacancy for six months, they won't sign up anyone for the military job that requires attending that course. They'll say that the skill is "closed."

When you first get in touch with a recruiter, expect to answer a lot of questions. Any recruiter wants to be able to contact you later by telephone or to mail material to your home. He'll also begin that screening process of figuring out how the military can use you and what you're looking for from the armed forces.

And, let's face it. You're also screening him.

WHAT HE'S LOOKING FOR

The recruiter is in the business of bringing people onto active duty. In another era, recruiters were only interested in filling quotas and convincing as many people as possible to sign on the magic line, raise their hands, and join the ranks of the U.S. armed forces. These days, recruiters are interested in the quality of recruits.

Every trainee represents a dollars-and-cents investment to the military, and the armed forces are becoming more reluctant to accept people who look "iffy." Not only does it cost thousands of dollars just to get someone to their first day of boot camp, but also there are a limited number of people who can attend basic training at any time. Sending a "long-shot" to boot camp may mean that a more qualified enlistee doesn't go and may decide to do something else after high school.

These are just a few factors that each recruiter has in mind during every conversation with a young person who is thinking about coming on active duty. Here are some of the things that a recruiter will want to know about you, starting with your first talk:

Are You a High School Graduate?

The military would prefer to enlist only people with high school diplomas. Partly that's because if everyone in boot camp is a graduate, then trainers can start their work at a higher level than when nongraduates are in the group.

But there's more to it than simple education. Having that diploma says something about you. It takes discipline to finish twelve years of schooling. People who don't graduate often don't have the self control necessary to be in the military. Their personal lives are a wreck, and they're not a good investment for the military, or for that matter for a civilian employer. Still, recruiters will accept a certain number of nongraduates. Those nongraduates shouldn't have anything else in their backgrounds that makes them look like gambles.

Are You Healthy?

On entering the military, everyone receives one of the most comprehensive physical examinations of their lives. But those exams cost money, and the government would prefer not to spend it if it's possible to detect folks with medical conditions that make them ineligible for military service. That early-screening job has fallen to the recruiters.

Do You Take Any Sort of Prescription Medicine?

Have you ever been hospitalized? Have you had seizures? Do you take insulin? Are you HIV positive? Expect these and many other questions about your health and medical history to pop up during your earliest conversations with a recruiter. Also, if you first contact a recruiter by telephone, expect the recruiter to push for a face-to-face meeting. Some medical problems, especially those involving weight, are difficult to discover by phone but very easy in person.

Do You Have Good Character?

By today's standards, the U.S. military has always been a "values-based" organization. The job of the armed forces—being so strong that no other power would dare attack this country and, once threatened, to prevail on the battlefield—is too important to be left to unreliable people.

For the military is the ultimate team, and recruiters need to know that the people coming on active duty don't have the sorts of personality problems that make them unlikely to become solid, reliable members of a larger organization. From the very first conversations with a potential enlistee, recruiters are trying to assess the character of people.

Yes, that may sound hokey, unscientific, and highly subjective, but that's what recruiters do. They want to ensure that the people they're bringing into uniform are the kind whom the recruiter wouldn't mind sharing a room with, working next to, or ultimately, having in the next foxhole on a battlefield.

Character counts in the military, and people who clearly don't have it will find themselves turned down or ignored. Specifically, recruiters look for:

- Drug and alcohol problems
- Problems with the law (including multiple traffic offenses)
- Liars.

The first two factors are clear; the third needs some explaining. Many fine people—including generals and admirals—had their brushes with the law growing up. Unfortunately, experimentation with alcohol is fairly common for many young people, as are illegal drugs. Recruiters don't expect to interview only angels. Some legal problems, escapades with alcohol, even some drug use can be overlooked when a person has a record that's otherwise good and the problems in question are clearly growing-up pains. There's some "give" there. But recruiters are tougher on people who misrepresent their backgrounds. They expect honesty from the men and women who come to them to join the military, and they can keep out people who lie about themselves.

WHAT DO YOU WANT TO DO?

Some people don't have a clear idea of what they want to do after they join the military. In fact, it is possible to enlist under rules that let the military decide later exactly what training and jobs you'll get. Most people want a say in deciding the things they'll do.

One of the responsibilities of a recruiter is to help applicants get what they want. Recruiters also guide people toward military jobs that rely upon their interests and skills. The military knows that the most productive, problem-free people are those who are doing exactly the things they want to do.

But it's not always possible to guarantee people the jobs and training they want. Assigning new military members to specific skills is often based upon tests. If the tests say a young man is not likely to do well in a particular active-duty job, the military won't sign him up for that job. The would-be soldier will have to pick another skill, try his luck with another branch of the armed forces, or give up his plans to enlist.

———— ✰ ————

Looking for a recruiter? Check your local telephone directory.
They're in the section for U.S. government offices, under Recruiting.
On the Internet, start with the main military Web page,
www.defenselink.mil. Follow the hyperlinks to the individual services,
and from there to each service's recruiting command.

When do you want to join? Remember that recruiters aren't interested solely in putting uniforms on a certain number of people each month. They're looking at what the military calls "the training pipeline," consisting of the classes after boot camp in which new military members learn the skills that they'll perform on active duty.

So timing becomes important. The recruiter is looking for people who will agree to come into the military at a particular moment that guarantees a steady flow of people from boot camp into the various skill-related training courses. By coming into the military later than they wish, many recruits can receive the training and assignments that they really want.

WHAT YOU'RE LOOKING FOR

Joining the military is a little like buying a car. Some negotiating is part of the experience. The salesman (in this case, the recruiter) wants to bring you into the military on terms that are most favorable to him and to the armed forces. The customer (in this case, you) has a few cards in his or her hand, the most important one being the ability to walk away.

What are some of the things you can ask for, and that the recruiter may be able to provide?

Guaranteed Skill

If you're going to spend a few years in uniform, you might as well spend it doing something that you want to do. Perhaps you want to do something that you're never again going to have the chance to do—like drive a tank or control the missiles that defend a ship. Or perhaps you want the military to give you training and experience in a skill that will improve your chances of getting a good job once you leave active duty.

You should know your military skill before you go to boot camp. But it won't come from the recruiter. At the Military Entrance Processing Station (MEPS), would-be recruits take aptitude tests that decide which training the military will let them take. At MEPS they sign a formal contract accepting that deal. The contract, not any promises made by a recruiter, are what cement a person's right to receive a certain kind of training.

But unless you sign up for a program in which you give the military the right to assign you to a skill after boot camp, you'll know your skill before boot camp. If the military offers a skill you don't want, you can walk away.

Bonuses

Not every job that the military has to offer is equally desirable in the eyes of potential enlistees. Some are dirty and dangerous. Others are identical to jobs done in the private sector, where the pay is better, separations from family are rare, and the lifestyle is more relaxed. To make the military more competitive in these situations, the government has authorized special bonuses to new recruits.

It's at this point that a recruiter isn't like a car salesman. The recruiter cannot decide who will get an enlistment bonus and who won't, nor can the recruiter decide the amount. Those details are controlled by the military's recruiting commands. Everyone who passes through the specific eligibility "hoops" gets the same bonus.

Fine Point: Enlistment bonuses are based upon hard-nosed decisions about what the military needs to do to bring enough people onto active duty with a certain mix of skills. From the military's standpoint, bonuses are used to fix problems. Once the problem is fixed, the bonus will go away. It's possible that a friend could receive a bonus one day for enlisting but you can't get it the next day, although you want to do the very same thing that your friend decided to do.

"Kickers"

Since many people join the military for its educational benefits, recruiters can sometimes offer more money for education as an enlistment inducement. This extra money is called "a kicker," and it's added to the regular educational payments under the Montgomery GI Bill. A kicker may take the form of an extra $400 a month in educational benefits, added to the usual $600 monthly total, giving you $1,000 a month to use in any way you see fit while enrolled in college or an approved training course.

Kickers are like bonuses. They're a tool that the military uses to fill manpower shortages. Kickers come and go, sometimes from day to day.

———————— ☆ ————————

"It's like joining a health spa—only they pay us."

—Bones Conway (Pauly Shore) in *In the Army Now*
(Hollywood Pictures, 1994)

———————————————

Guaranteed Assignment

If you agree to sign on the magic line, sometimes the military will promise to send you to a specific place after your military training is done. You might want to go to Germany or Korea, or you might want to be assigned to a base down the road from your folks. Sometimes recruiters can do that. If that's one of the things you want, make sure you have that promise in writing.

But guaranteed assignments are one of the "softest" incentives offered to bring people into uniform. Even the best-intentioned recruiter and the clearest written promise won't keep you out of an international hot spot. If the military needs you anywhere in the world, it will send you there, regardless of guaranteed assignments.

Time (Duration)

When people join the military, they take on a legal obligation to serve for a specific number of years. The length of time a new service member has to spend is something that's worked out between the recruiter and the recruit. Each branch of the military has minimum periods that people must serve, usually two years or four years. Often, for agreeing to serve longer than the minimum, people can get bonuses, the best assignments, or special training. The length of military service is an item heavily controlled by military regulations, and recruiters don't always have much freedom of choice.

Time (Starting)

How long after reaching an agreement with a recruiter are folks expected to show up at boot camp? That's another subject that's worked out between recruiters and recruits. It can be a few days, or it can be more than a year. That decision usually hangs upon the availability of an empty chair in the training course that follows boot camp, the one that trains new military members in the specific skills they'll be using on active duty.

The military's name for the formal program for late-starters is the "Delayed Entry Program," or DEP (rhymes with "step").

Extra Stripes

Normally, military rank isn't negotiable. But it may be possible to start your military career with one or two extra stripes on your shoulder. The extra rank can come for signing up for a specific skill, by persuading friends to go to the recruiter, or agreeing to talk about your experiences at assemblies in your old high school. Recruiters have considerable latitude with this benefit, since not everyone is cut out to be a salesman (or an unofficial recruiter).

THE DON'T-WORRY-ABOUT-IT LIST

The most important military benefits are written into federal law. They go to everyone in uniform. Recruiters can neither give, take away, nor change them. Some of the things that a recruiter cannot affect are:

Pay Scale

Everyone with the same rank, who has been in uniform for the same time, receives the same minimum pay. Extra money can be added for skills and assignments.

Family Benefits

Recruiters can neither give nor take away any government benefit for your spouse or children. Those things are written into law, set by regulations, or delegated to base commanders.

Medical Coverage

If you wear the uniform, you will receive free treatment for any medical problem, including injuries that arise off base and off duty.

GI Bill Education

With the exception of "kickers," discussed earlier in this chapter, nothing a recruiter does or doesn't do affects payments for schooling.

GI Bill Home Loans

Ditto. Everything about the program of government help in buying a home is beyond the control of recruiters.

Insurance Coverage

Everyone on active duty can—and should—sign up for a government-backed life insurance program. Nothing done in the recruiting office can affect this benefit.

★ ★ 5 ★ ★

OTHER MILITARY OPTIONS

In our look at joining the military, we've talked about active-duty enlistments. The majority of people who decide to commit a few years of their lives to the armed forces enter as active-duty enlistees. But in the military, an "active-duty enlistment" is a very specific thing. It means a person begins full-time service with an enlisted rank. But there are other paths that lead to a uniform.

Not everyone in the military does it as a full-time job. Men and women in the reserves and the National Guard are in the military, too. They are paid to train one weekend each month and two weeks each year—using the same pay scale as the active-duty folks—and they can qualify for a military retirement after twenty years' service. Increasingly, they are called upon to leave their full-time civilian jobs and help the armed forces in overseas hot spots.

Another way of joining the military is as an officer. Officers are the managers, the commanders, the people who are ultimately responsible for everyone in uniform and everything that's done. With few exceptions, officers are college graduates. They have their own training courses, which produce military-related skills. They are paid more than enlisted people, but they are under more pressure to prove that they're earning their pay. Officers serve on active duty and as part-time soldiers in the reserves and National Guard.

Although the rest of this book will keep the focus upon active-duty enlistments, in this chapter we're going to pause to examine those two other options for joining the military—the "weekend warrior" and the officer.

As always, the best way to start is by looking at the military through the eyes of a person who is already in it.

BRYAN'S STORY: A LITTLE-USED PATH
FOR BECOMING AN OFFICER

Bryan Salmon looks like he stepped from a recruiting poster—red haired, lean, quick to smile—a high school jock with brains.

For a couple of years, he's had a military job that is hands-down glamorous. He is a pilot in the United States Air Force. When Salmon goes to work, he sits behind the controls of the nation's top-of-the-line jet fighter, the single-seat F-15.

A native of Colorado Springs, he belongs to an elite brotherhood, the modern version of the ancient knights, who engage in single-handed combat eight miles above the ground in a plane that can travel more than 1,000 miles an hour. Already, he has thirty-two combat missions under his belt patrolling the no-fly zone in Iraq, and he's under orders for a tour in Japan.

It almost didn't happen. "When I was in high school, I was the kid who only wanted to play sports," he said. His grades weren't bad, but his SAT scores weren't good enough to get into a really top-notch school.

Fortunately, his athletic ability drew the attention of coaches at the U.S. Air Force Academy. They offered him a little-known deal—enlist in the Air Force, and they'd send him to prep school for a year. If he proved there that he could meet the academy's demanding standards, he could win a highly coveted spot at the U.S. Air Force Academy.

Salmon knew he was being handed a once-in-a-lifetime opportunity. He grabbed it for all it was worth, hitting the books hard, doing more than just catching up on math and English. For the first time, he learned how to learn.

He graduated from the prep school, entered the Air Force Academy, and did well enough to be among the 225 new lieutenants selected in a class of 1,200 to attend flight school after graduation.

----------- ☆ -----------

"What is this place? Is it, maybe, a prison or a loony house?"

"This is the United States Military Academy."

—Marty Maher (Tyrone Power) and Rudy Heinz
(Peter Graves) in *The Long Gray Line*
(Columbia Pictures, 1955)

In the Air Force—and the other services, as well—only officers pilot the modern, multimillion-dollar aircraft that make up the U.S. military's aerial fleet. Being selected for flight school wasn't the end of Bryan's studying. It was the beginning.

From the beginning of flight school—actually, the first of three different flight schools—to the beginning of his first assignment as an Air Force pilot took nearly two and a half years.

"I still think it's cool when people ask what I do and I tell them I'm a pilot," he said. "But they don't see me coming in to work at six in the morning or leaving at six at night. Actually flying is only a small part of my job."

A typical hour-long flight will consume most of a day, what with flight planning, preflight briefings, preflight inspections, then a variety of post-flight briefings, inspections, and critiques.

"I've had people come up and say it must be nice to come to work, fly around, then go home."

Bryan Salmon learned at prep school that hard work was the key to getting what he wanted. Now he's learning that more hard work is necessary to keep doing what he loves.

THE PART-TIME MILITARY

Only about half of the people in the military are on full-time service. For every person who wears a uniform of the armed forces every day, there is another person who only puts it on for two days every month. These are the members of the reserves and the National Guard, which together are called the "reserve components."

Reservists and Guardsmen are paid using the same pay scale as the active-duty force. They are eligible for medical care and many on-base benefits, such as exchanges and commissaries. Under certain conditions, they can get educational benefits under the Montgomery GI Bill and help buying a home under the GI Bill's home-loan program. If they serve for twenty years, they can receive a military retirement, although the reserve-component retirement is computed using formulas that aren't as generous as the ones used for active-duty people.

A typical reserve-component member is assigned to a unit that meets for two days every month, plus two weeks every year. The two-week period is informally known as "summer camp," although it can come at any time during the year. Some reservists and guardsmen—usually officers and high-skill enlisted—can perform duties by themselves, without being a member of a unit. These folks must receive the okay from their parent service to do this, and approval doesn't come often for folks new to the military.

The military likes to see people who enlist in the reserves and National Guard first go to boot camp and then to their skill-related training before returning to the civilian world and taking an assignment with a reserve-component unit. That can be an investment of at least six months' time. However, if recruiters have trouble finding enough new reservists and guardsmen, they can come up with a better deal.

Sometimes, the Army will let new reservists go to boot camp one summer, return to their civilian world, then go to skill-training the next summer, then return to their civilian life. The Marines have a program that breaks that down over three summers.

The men and women at the local military recruiter's office may—or may not—be able to sign someone up for an enlistment in the reserves. To find out if a recruiter can do that, ask a direct question. If the answer is "no," ask the recruiter for the name and telephone number of the nearest reserve recruiter. Expect a little resistance, because the recruiter will want to talk you into coming on active duty.

The National Guard has its recruiters. Any military recruiter should be able to give you a telephone number for those folks. You can also call the state headquarters of the National Guard. It's in the state capital. Some telephone listings are under "adjutant general," which is the title for the state commander.

Trivia: What's the difference between the reserves and the National Guard? Not much any more. A state governor can order National Guardsmen—but not reservists—to duty for such things as riots and national disasters.

ROUTE 1 TO OFFICERS' INSIGNIA: ACADEMIES

If you want to make a career of the military, many folks would advise you to go as an officer. They're the ones with the authority, pay, and control over their own careers. The best way to become an officer is to attend one of the military academies. Graduates receive such an intensive training on military issues—and such a top-notch education—that they end up rising to the top of the profession of arms.

Lots of schools have "academy" in their names. In this subchapter, we're going to look at the top four—the U.S. Military Academy at West Point (Army), the U.S. Naval Academy at Annapolis (Navy and Marine Corps), the U.S. Air Force Academy in Colorado Springs, and the U.S. Coast Guard Academy in New London, Connecticut. The other schools that call

———— ★ ————

Don't call reservists and National Guardsmen "weekend warriors."
Some consider it an insult.

———————————

themselves academies are essentially ROTC programs, and we'll look at ROTC later in this chapter.

The military academies are four-year colleges at which students—called "plebes" at West Point and the Air Force Academy, while the naval and Coast Guard academies call them "midshipmen"—earn both a recognized bachelor's degree and a commission as officers. While at school, all expenses are paid by the government, including health care, and they receive about $600 a month (year 2000 rate). They must spend at least five years on active duty after graduating.

The Army, Navy and Air Force have systems in which applicants are technically "nominated" for the academy by a member of Congress. The Coast Guard makes selections on a competitive basis. Nominations can mean that people who are politically connected have an advantage in getting into the academies. Most members of Congress, however, make their nominations purely by the numbers. Everyone must meet certain criteria. They must be:

- U.S. citizens
- At least 17
- No older than twenty-two
- Able to meet standards in academics, fitness, and moral character
- Single
- Not legally obligated to support anyone, including parents.

Special rules that bypass the normal nominating process and make it easier to win acceptance at one of the academies apply to people who fall within other categories, including:

- Child of a military parent
- Child of disabled veteran, military retiree, or veteran who died from service-related cause
- Enlisted members of military
- ROTC cadets
- Child of Medal of Honor holder.

Folks interested in applying for a military academy should be in the spring of their junior year in high school. Ask for an application from your member of Congress or directly from the academy.

The Army, Navy and Air Force have preparatory schools for their academies. (Marines attend the Naval Academy Preparatory School.) Each prep school offers a one-year period of full-time academic study, on active duty. The idea is to take enlisted people who don't quite have the academic credentials for an academy—usually athletes—and spend a year in the classroom bringing them up to standards. Prep school graduates aren't guaranteed appointments to the academies. In fact, those coming into uniform to attend the prep school must agree to spend eight years in the reserves or National Guard if they're not picked for the military academy.

Fine Point: A nomination to a military academy isn't a guaranteed acceptance. Normally each member of Congress can have five constituents at any time at each academy, and the lawmakers can nominate ten people for each vacancy. Academy officials select who's going, from the list of nominations.

ROUTE 2 TO OFFICERS' INSIGNIA: ROTC AND PLC

The majority of people wearing the insignia of officers started out in ROTC (Reserve Officer Training Corps) programs at civilian colleges or universities. There, in addition to their regular college courses, they added a couple hours of classroom instruction each week and, typically, an afternoon on the parade field. The government provides uniforms and other gear at no cost to ROTC students.

Everyone in the final two years of ROTC receives a token monthly payment ($150 in year 2000). They are obligated to attend one summer camp—usually between their junior and senior years of college—which lasts about two months and which is the equivalent of boot camp. After graduating with their bachelor's degrees, these ROTC cadets and midshipmen formally become officers, a process known as "commissioning." They assume a legal obligation to spend a certain amount of time—six or eight years—as a member either of a reserve component or on active duty.

The first step in joining an ROTC program involves being accepted by a school that offers ROTC. Not every college does. If you later drop out of school, you also drop out of ROTC.

In many schools, the ROTC program is open to most people in reasonably good health. At the start of the last two years, the physical standards are tightened, and anyone with medical problems, criminal records, or other things in their backgrounds that would prevent them from serving in the military are also kept out of ROTC.

Scholarships are available to ROTC students. Amounts vary by service. Accepting a scholarship can obligate a student to spend additional time in the military after commissioning.

The Marine Corps has a program called the "Platoon Leaders Course," or PLC, which is similar in some respects to ROTC. Participants in both programs attend fully accredited institutions of higher learning and end up receiving an officer's commission upon graduation. But in PLC, participants don't attend classes and drill periods throughout the year. Instead, they attend intensive summer training camps between their academic years. They are eligible for $150 a month scholarships. The program carries a minimum obligation of three and a half years on active duty.

ROUTE 3 TO OFFICERS' INSIGNIA: OTS AND OCS

For a number of reasons, some people with the potential to be good officers don't attend an academy or ROTC. The military still wants them. For them, the services offer "Officer Candidate School," or OCS, ("Officer Training School," OTS, in the Air Force), a special path to an officer's bars.

OCS and OTS are open to college graduates. Once selected, participants spend their first three months in the military attending a special school that combines elements of boot camp with the basic instruction needed to be officers.

The Army and the Marine Corps have programs offering commissions to people without four-year college degrees. The Army's route is through its regular OCS program, while the Marines have a slightly different program called the Meritorious Commissioning Program. Both efforts have a huge piece of fine print: the only nongraduates who can sign up are people already on active duty or in the reserves. You can't come into the Army or the Marine Corps as a nongraduate and go straight to OCS.

Important: Recruiters can bring people onto active duty with the promise of going to OCS or OTS. Or they sign someone up for the military, explain the rules for getting into those commissioning programs, and wish them luck. Don't confuse information and good wishes with a guarantee.

Also important: Anyone signing up for OCS or OTS should have a "Plan B," an idea of what happens if things go poorly. If you don't pass the precommissioning course, will you be discharged or will you be obligated to spend a certain number of years in the military as an enlisted person? Both things can happen.

ROUTE 4 TO OFFICER'S INSIGNIA: THE PROFESSIONAL PATH

Did you know that the U.S. military has its own medical school? Or that the armed forces give scholarships to people to attend medical school? Or that folks with law and theological degrees can come directly into uniform as officers?

Like everything involving the military, these routes to an officer's insignia have their own eligibility rules, which are subject to change. In most instances, recruiters are not involved in explaining the rules or in taking applications. But recruiters should be able to provide an important service to folks interested in these programs. Recruiters should be able to say where people can go to find out more information. Usually that will involve a mailing address, a telephone number, or an Internet address.

Here are some details about a variety of programs that enable people to start their military careers as officers:

Direct Commissions

Those who have already finished their professional education and meet their profession's criteria for certification can enter the military as officers. They don't have to start at the lowest officer rank, either. This program for starting out as an officer is called a "direct commission." Physicians, dentists, lawyers and chaplains are the major professions eligible for direct commissions.

Military's Medical School

On the grounds of the Navy's famed Bethesda medical center outside Washington, D.C., the armed forces run their own medical school. Called the Uniformed Services University of Health Sciences, it is a full-scale, four-year, fully accredited institution producing physicians and other health-care Ph.D.s.

Students are second lieutenants (Army and Air Force) or ensigns (Navy or Coast Guard) while enrolled. Tuition, books and other equipment are

———————— ✮ ————————

"Don't get sore at Irving, fella. He's had ROTC."

—Will Stockdale (Andy Griffith) in
No Time for Sergeants (Warner Brothers, 1958)

free. Upon graduation, new doctors become captains (Army or Air Force) or lieutenant commanders (Navy or Coast Guard). They must spend at least seven years on active duty. That obligation increases if the new doctors are given time after graduating for internships and residency programs to sharpen their professional skills.

Applicants can be civilians or people already on active duty. Like for any medical school, admissions are competitive and very tough. Only the people with the best high-school records and the top scores in admission tests are accepted.

Health Scholarships

Students in regular medical schools can qualify for financial help from the military, in exchange for a legal commitment to spend some time— usually, at least three years—in uniform after graduation.

The largest program is the Armed Forces Health Professionals Scholarship Program. It covers people in school for medicine, dentistry, psychology and optometry. The military pays for tuition, books and related fees, in addition to giving participants an allowance of about $1,000 a month. During summer breaks in studies, participants may have to spend up to forty-five days on active duty as second lieutenants (Army or Air Force) or ensigns (Navy or Coast Guard).

Besides this Defense Department scholarship program, the Army has another effort that gives scholarships to medical and dental school graduates who are enrolled in studies called "residency" programs. Known as the Financial Assistance Program, it provides about $20,000 a year for educational expenses, plus another $1,000 a month for living expenses. These were the rates for the year 2000, and they're likely to increase.

★ ★ 6 ★ ★

MAKING YOUR PICK

One of the most important decisions that faces everyone who joins the military has very few guidelines: Which branch of the armed forces should you join?

Is it better to be all that you can be and join the Army? How about becoming one of the few, the proud, the Marines? If you want an adventure, not a job, you can sign up for the Air Force. Or you can join the Navy and see the world, or perhaps you want the Coast Guard, where the thrill of serving your country is combined with the knowledge you're helping to save lives.

The question of picking a branch of the military to join, whether on active duty or as a member of the reserves or National Guard, doesn't have any right or wrong answers. The basic benefits going to military personnel—and later to veterans—are uniformly applied to all members of the military. They don't depend upon the color of your uniform.

As we've done several times during our look at the experience of joining the military, let's hear from someone who's gone through it recently.

JESSICA'S STORY: PICKING A SERVICE AND A CAREER

On her way to becoming an FBI agent, Jessica Acosta found herself in the uniform of a Marine Corps officer.

Along the way, the idea of belonging to a tradition that includes such names as Tarawa and Iwo Jima began to look more important than another illustrious tradition, with names like John Dillinger and J. Edgar Hoover.

"During the last few months, seeing what the Marine Corps has to offer, I've been wondering why I would want to leave it," said Jessica, a petite woman who is quick to smile. She's not the type you'd expect to be nationally ranked as a freestyle wrestler in school.

A native of Tehachapi, California, she started thinking seriously about spending a few years in uniform during her sophomore year at California State University at Bakersfield. At that time, the goal was to become an FBI agent. Dreaming about any career isn't enough. You have to take slow, steady steps toward it.

Jessica had researched the requirements for becoming an FBI agent and discovered that the FBI wants its agents to have at least three years experience after graduation from college before they apply.

Where would she like to work for those three years? What could she do in just three years, as a new college graduate, that would strengthen her chances for getting into the FBI? What impresses an FBI agent?

Jessica knew what impressed her. Her father, a long-haul truck driver, had spent four years as a young man in the Marine Corps. That was the perfect idea. She would get training in weapons and physical fitness. (Remember, being an FBI agent isn't a desk job.) She could prove she was disciplined and knew how to handle responsibility.

Her recruiter pointed out that as a college graduate she would be eligible to become an officer. So Jessica became a Marine.

She went to Officer's Candidate School, the officer's version of basic training, for ten weeks between her junior and senior years. After graduation she would officially become an officer and went on active duty for further training.

This option let her concentrate on her studies. There were no military-related courses during the year in college (as in ROTC), nor were her weekends taken away from studies (which happens when you join the reserves or the National Guard).

Most young people on active duty have stories to tell about the recruiters who called them regularly and even visited their homes once they

---

★

"There's something wrong with us. Something very, very, very seriously wrong with us. We're soldiers."

—John Winger (Bill Murray) in *Stripes*
(Columbia Pictures, 1981)

———— ⭐ ————

"The first thing you have to understand about this ship is that she
was designed by geniuses to be run by idiots."

—Lt. Keefer (Fred MacMurray) in *The Caine Mutiny*
(Columbia Pictures, 1954)

showed an interest in the military. Jessica's experience with recruiters was
different.

"If you want to be an officer, you have to show the interest," she said.
"The recruiters will give you all the time you need, but first you've got to
show the interest."

HOW SOME PEOPLE PICK

Jessica's story highlights the two most important factors that people
consider in deciding whether to join the Army, Navy, Air Force, Marine
Corps or Coast Guard—family history and the best offer from a recruiter.

If your father was in the Navy, the odds are that you grew up with
some sort of attachment to the Navy and not to the other branches of the
military. That's human nature. It's also human for you to be more likely to
join the Navy than one of the other services. Yes, that may be a tad sentimental, but who says sentiment is always bad? If you and your father
went through the same experiences in the military, even if they come
decades apart, that should bring you closer today. You may even find that
some of the things your father learned decades ago in the Navy may still
be useful.

The other way to decide is to pick the service whose recruiter offers you
the training, career field, or assignment that you want. If learning to repair
helicopters is the dream of your life, does it really matter whether you repair helicopters for the Army, Navy, Air Force, Marine Corps, or Coast

———— ⭐ ————

"I've got the sky, the smell of jet exhaust, my bike."

—Topper Harley (Charlie Sheen) in *Hot Shots*
(Twentieth Century Fox, 1991)

Guard? All do it. But not all may be willing to guarantee that training when you're ready to receive it.

Many people find that their career field affects their life in uniform more than their branch of the military. Will you have to spend a lot of time away from the United States? Depends. There are people in the Navy who don't leave home, and there are people in the other services who pop from one international hot spot to another.

THINGS THAT CAN CHANGE BETWEEN SERVICES

Each branch of the armed forces follows the same basic rules for treating military people and their families. Federal law and overall policy of the Department of Defense set down the framework for most military benefits and the policies that affect the lives of people in uniform. Still, there can be some differences between services, particularly between people in different career fields.

Promotions

For lower-ranking officers and enlisted members, the promotion rate is usually automatic. After so many months in uniform, if they haven't had any disciplinary problems, they are advanced to the next rank. That pace isn't always the same for all branches of the military. A recruiter can give you the latest information for his service's promotion rate.

Assignments

If you want the military to assign you near your parents in Wyoming, it's probably not wise to enlist in the Navy; naval bases tend to be located on the coast (although there are exceptions). Each branch of the military has its own installations, both here and overseas, and most people in uniform are stationed at one of them. If it's important that the mil-

---- ★ ----

"Takes a certain kind of sadistic temperament to be a Marine."

—Buddusky (Jack Nicholson) in *The Last Detail*
(Columbia Pictures, 1973)

itary assign you to a particular location, state, or region, make sure you're joining one of the armed forces that actually has installations there.

Away from Home

A fact of military life is that sometimes people in uniform are sent to places where they are separated from their families, especially in other countries or aboard ship. That can happen to anyone in any service. For people new to the military, it's probably most likely for members of the Navy and least likely for those in the Coast Guard.

★ ★ 7 ★ ★

APTITUDE TESTS

At one time, joining the military was simple. You signed on the dotted line, then passed a physical that was no more complicated that proving you had ten fingers and a heartbeat. These days things are more complicated. Recruits are determined to have a voice in selecting the jobs they're willing to do. The military is also more finicky than it was when the grandfathers of today's recruits first put on their uniforms. Many active-duty skills demand aptitudes that not everyone possesses, and there's the question of motivation. The folks running today's armed services understand that people perform best when they're doing jobs that interest them and that they feel they can handle.

To provide the right match between recruit and job, the military has spent years and tens of millions of dollars to refine tests to identify both the skills and the interests of would-be recruits. The personnel experts in the armed forces know exactly which kinds of people do best in which jobs, and they can back up their predictions with decades of solid research.

The heart of the military's testing program is the Armed Services Vocational Aptitude Battery, or ASVAB. It's called a "battery" because it's actually a series of tests administered at one time to answer a host of questions: What do you really want to do with your working life? What jobs are you most prepared to handle? What skills do you have the greatest likelihood of mastering?

In fact, the ASVAB is such an effective tool for students thinking about their career options that more than fourteen thousand high schools offer the test to everyone. The military sees the ASVAB as a key ingredient of a "career exploration program," and many high school guidance counselors agree. The test has an importance far beyond the military. For those thinking about enlisting, however, the ASVAB is an investment that will shape much about their years in uniform.

THE BASICS ON THE ASVAB

The test takes one hour. In the past, it's been taken with pencil and paper (which takes three hours) but increasingly it's moving to self-paced computer programs. Everyone who takes the test receives several scores that show their aptitudes and interests, along with several booklets that help them interpret the results.

Like the college admission tests, books are commercially available that help people "cram" for an ASVAB test. Both recruiters and guidance counselors say that isn't necessary, although those books may be helpful in giving people an idea of what the actual test will look like.

Also like the college admission tests, the ASVAB is tightly controlled. Usually, it's given at one time and one place to everyone who's going to take it, although some large high schools have more than one testing day. Still, no one can buy an ASVAB test. No one can walk into a guidance counselor's office and ask to take it.

The military gives the same ASVAB test as the guidance counselors. Like high school officials, military officials control the times and places that tests are administered.

Whether an ASVAB test is arranged by a guidance counselor or a recruiter, some things are always the same. There is no charge. Taking the test incurs no obligation to join the military. It will not affect high school grades. For that matter, the ASVAB isn't something anyone can fail. Because it matches interests and aptitudes with specific careers, the ASVAB makes everyone a winner.

THE ASVAB AND THE MILITARY

The military uses the ASVAB to make two important decisions. First, it's used to decide who will be allowed to enlist. People who score too low can't come on active duty. Second, the test is used to decide career fields and training. All the offers of jobs and courses by recruiters as incentives to get people to join usually have big "ifs" attached. Recruits can get the training and the assignments they want *if* they score high enough on the ASVAB tests. Recruiters are the gatekeepers for the ASVAB. They decide when people interested in the military will take the test.

——————— ✭ ———————

"This guy is smart, very smart. He has an IQ."

—Sgt. Bilko (Steve Martin) in *Sgt. Bilko*
(Universal Studios, 1996)

That computerized test is scored instantly, and people learn immediately—sometimes only a few minutes after taking it—which assignments and training the military will allow them to get.

When people take the ASVAB at a MEPS facility, it's usually part of an all-day processing that ends with the official oath of enlistment. To eliminate unpleasant surprises, some recruiters will let folks take an old ASVAB test in the recruiter's office. The results of that test are unofficial, but they will let both recruiter and recruit know what's likely to happen as a result of taking the official test at a MEPS facility.

People going directly into the National Guard or the reserves at an enlisted rank must also take ASVAB. Normally, people in a program that will bring them into the military as an officer don't have to take the test, although many people find it a useful tool in sorting out their personal interests and professional options.

Anyone who took an ASVAB test at their high schools during their junior or senior years may not have to retake it. Usually, the results are good for two years.

THE TEST

The Armed Services Vocational Aptitude Battery consists of more than three hundred questions, organized in ten different tests. All answers are multiple choice. Those ten tests are:

- Word knowledge
- Paragraph comprehension
- Arithmetic reasoning
- Mathematics knowledge
- General science
- Auto and shop information
- Mechanical comprehension
- Electronics information

- Numerical operations
- Coding speed.

Each of the tests is individually timed. Participants receive a total score and scores for each of the ten tests. Three other scores—verbal, math, and academic ability—are derived from combinations of the ten test results. Here are some sample questions:

General Science

1. An eclipse of the sun throws the shadow of the
   A. moon on the sun
   B. moon on the earth
   C. earth on the sun
   D. earth on the moon

2. Substances which hasten chemical reaction time without themselves undergoing changes are called
   A. buffers
   B. colloids
   C. reducers
   D. catalysts

Arithmetic Reasoning

3. How many 36-passenger buses will it take to carry 144 people?
   A. 3
   B. 4
   C. 5
   D. 6

4. It costs $0.50 per square yard to waterproof canvas. What will it cost to waterproof a canvas truck cover that is 15′ × 24′?
   A. $6.67

"First thing that Fleet Academy looks at is your math score."

—Carmen Ibanez (Denise Richards) in
Starship Troopers (Columbia Pictures, 1997)

B. $18.00

C. $20.00

D. $180.00

Word Knowledge

5. The wind is variable today.

    A. mild

    B. steady

    C. shifting

    D. chilling

6. Rudiments most nearly means

    A. politics

    B. minute details

    C. promotion opportunities

    D. basic methods and procedures

Paragraph Comprehension

7. Twenty-five percent of all household burglaries can be attributed to unlocked windows or doors. Crime is the result of opportunity plus desire. To prevent crime, it is each individual's responsibility to

    A. provide the desire

    B. provide the opportunity

    C. prevent the desire

    D. prevent the opportunity

8. In certain areas, water is so scarce that every attempt is made to conserve it. For instance, on an oasis in the Sahara Desert the amount of water necessary for each date palm has been carefully determined. How much water is each tree given?

    A. No water at all

    B. Water on alternate days

    C. Exactly the amount required

    D. Water only if it is healthy

Numerical Operations

9. $3 + 9 =$

    A. 3

B. 6

C. 12

D. 13

10. 60/15 =

A. 3

B. 4

C. 5

D. 6

Coding Speed

If the word "bargain" = 8385, "game" = 6456, "knife" = 7150, "sunshine" = 7489, "point" = 4703, "chin" = 8930, "house" = 2859, "music" = 1117, "owner" = 6227, "sofa" = 9645, then

11. "Game" is

A. 6456

B. 7150

C. 8385

D. 8930

E. 9645

12. "Knife" is

A. 1117

B. 6456

C. 7150

D. 7489

E. 8385

13. "Bargain" is

A. 2859

B. 6227

C. 7489

D. 8385

E. 9645

14. "Chin" is

A. 2859

B. 4703

C. 8385

D. 8930

E. 9645

15. "House" is
   A. 1117
   B. 2859
   C. 6227
   D. 7150
   E. 7489

16. "Sofa" is
   A. 7150
   B. 7489
   C. 8385
   D. 8930
   E. 9645

17. "Owner" is
   A. 4703
   B. 6227
   C. 6456
   D. 7150
   E. 8930

Auto and Shop Information

18. A car uses too much oil when which parts are worn?
   A. pistons
   B. piston rings
   C. main bearings
   D. connecting rods

19. A chisel is used for
   A. prying
   B. cutting
   C. twisting
   D. grinding

———— ☆ ————

"The trouble with you is that when you get a command,
it never goes north of your neck."

—Francis (himself) in *Francis Goes to West Point*
(Universal Studios, 1952)

Mathematics Knowledge

20. If $X + 6 = 7$, then X is equal to
    A. -1
    B. 0
    C. 1
    D. $7/6$

21. What is the area of a square that is five feet long on one side?
    A. 1 square foot
    B. 5 square feet
    C. 10 square feet
    D. 25 square feet

Electronics Information

22. Which of the following has the least resistance?
    A. wood
    B. iron
    C. rubber
    D. silver

OTHER TOOLS

Everyone who takes the ASVAB at a high school should receive a special pamphlet: *Exploring Careers: The ASVAB Workbook*. It links ASVAB scores to careers in both the military and the private sector.

Another invaluable publication tied to the ASVAB is the *Occupational Outlook Handbook*, a Department of Labor publication that lays out in clear detail the skills and training needed for hundreds of civilian and military jobs. Most guidance counselors and many public libraries have this publication.

For those on a purely military track, *Military Careers*, a Defense Department publication, is an invaluable reference. It gives simple explanations of what folks in different military jobs do, as well as the training they receive and their civilian counterparts. This book is also available from guidance counselors and public libraries.

★ ★ 8 ★ ★

MILITARY ENTRANCE PROCESSING STATION

Between the recruiter and the drill instructor, there's an important step on the way to joining the military. It's called the Military Entrance Processing Station, or MEPS (rhymes with "steps"). That's where would-be recruits find out if they meet the military's physical standards. It's also the place where people take the ASVAB. Most importantly, MEPS is where future soldiers, sailors, airmen, Marines and Coast Guardsmen raise their hands and recite the oath that legally makes them members of the United States armed forces.

MEPS can be an important tool for people who are about to join the military. It's staffed by active-duty people who are experts in all sorts of areas pertaining to enlistment and the benefits of military service. For people wondering about the promises made by recruiters, MEPS is the place where they can get the gold-plated, final word. In fact, they'll find themselves questioned repeatedly at MEPS to find out if a recruiter has made unwritten promises.

Everyone who enlists in the military will pass through a MEPS. Usually, people in the various programs that result in commissioning as officers don't attend a MEPS.

A visit to the MEPS is an intense, one-day experience. Representatives from all the services will be there to guide people through a seemingly endless number of forms that must be filled out, tests that must be completed, group sessions that must be attended, and one-on-one counseling sessions that will be scheduled. The military personnel running the MEPS aren't drill instructors. They won't raise their voices or criticize anyone.

Still, most would-be recruits will get a touch of the military's impersonality at the MEPS.

Here's how that special, little-known part of the enlistment process looks to one woman who spends a lot of her time there.

NANCY'S STORY: FROM SOVIET SUBS TO NEW RECRUITS

When she started out in the military, Nancy Holcomb spent a lot of time in places that people didn't know were naval bases, tracking Soviet submarines by the tell-tale underwater noises that they made.

In recent years, she's been following a more interesting "target"—the young men and women who are thinking about joining one of the armed forces.

"Young people today have so many options out there for them. It's easy for them to get confused," said Nancy, who now lives in Spokane, Washington.

She grew up in Dixon, Illinois, the hometown of Pres. Ronald Reagan. The daughter of a fences-and-awning salesman, she was on the fast track at high school, graduating when she was only sixteen.

Nancy wanted the Navy. But the Navy doesn't want sixteen-year-olds. "I hounded my recruiter constantly for over two years so he'd know that I was serious." She spent those years in a community college.

When she was old enough to enlist, she found herself on a waiting list. "One Friday, the recruiter called me, said that a young lady had dropped out, and told me to be ready to go that Monday." Even though she had already registered at a four-year college—and had made a non-refundable down payment on her tuition—Nancy went.

"I'll never forget when my recruiter came by my house at 3:30 in the morning to pick me up. My mother was standing on the porch in her bathrobe, crying."

Nancy's recruiter drove her to a military processing center in Chicago. "It was huge. There were lots of other men and women being herded through it. I took my physical exams with eighteen other women. It was exciting and scary for a small-town girl from rural Illinois."

------------ ★ ------------

"They don't speak my language around here. And I don't speak theirs."

—Chris Winters (John Payne) in *To the Shores of Tripoli*
(Twentieth Century Fox, 1942)

Little did Nancy know at the time that she would end up commanding the same kind of processing center, years later.

The Navy trained her to be an "ocean systems technician." During the height of the cold war, these specialists, called "OTs," worked in facilities on shore to track the vast Soviet submarine fleet. Much of their data came from ships towing underwater arrays that picked up the noises of submarines.

"It was an exciting job. You couldn't expect the same thing to happen when you went to work."

Her first assignment was at a small shoreside facility in Delaware next to a state park. It was so quiet and out of the way that many of the people who lived in the area didn't know that the Navy was in their neighborhood.

That job was followed by a stint on Midway Island in the Pacific. She was one of a handful of female sailors among an active-duty population of about 350.

"It was like being on an island with a lot of brothers," Nancy said.

After Midway, she went back to college to get the first of three degrees (she now has a bachelor's and two master's) and became an officer.

She has been in charge of 150 recruiters in Chicago. Now a lieutenant commander (equivalent to a major in other services), she commands the MEPS in Spokane.

A visit to the MEPS as a would-be recruit can be a stressful event. That's when the idea of joining the military and all it entails—leaving family, leaving home, stepping into a new way of life—can suddenly become real.

"We are careful to be professional in our handling of all people. We want to make sure we treat everyone with respect."

Although she has more than two decades in uniform, Nancy still speaks with enthusiasm when she talks about being on active duty. It's not difficult for her to be enthusiastic.

"I love it," she says. "In twenty-three years, I can honestly say that I haven't had a bad tour [of duty]. It's a great way of life."

MEPS BASICS

Going to a MEPS center is an integral part of working with a recruiter. It's the recruiter who arranges a visit.

A visit to the MEPS starts before dawn. For that reason, the military arranges for most people to stay at a motel near the MEPS facility. The government pays for their lodging, plus an evening meal and a breakfast. Potential recruits usually end up sharing a room with another person scheduled to go to the MEPS. Sometimes, as happened with Nancy

Holcomb, the recruiter will personally take folks to the motel or the MEPS facility.

The night before a visit to a MEPS facility is the wrong time to celebrate, since blood tests and breathalyzer tests will be taken. These days, the military isn't interested in people who have drinking problems. People with measurable amounts of alcohol in their systems could find themselves permanently barred from military service.

A good night's rest is the best last-minute preparation for a MEPS visit. Be warned that everyone spends some time standing around the MEPS in their underwear. Avoid underwear that might be embarrassing. But wear something. People who don't wear underwear—and that includes bras for women—will find their tests abruptly ended. Shoes are necessary, too.

MEPS facilities, like boot camps, are zero-tobacco zones. No smoking, dipping or chewing.

People sent to a MEPS facility are expected to stay there until the processing ends, usually in late afternoon. The military provides free lunches, and vending machines are usually available for snacks throughout the day.

Not too long ago, people went to a military processing center with their bags packed for boot camp. If they passed the various examinations, they walked out of the processing center and stepped into buses that took them to basic training.

Today, there is a lag of at least three or four days between a MEPS visit and leaving home for boot camp. For people who join under the Delayed Entry Program, or DEP, that interval can be many months.

A DAY AT MEPS

The exact schedule varies from one MEPS facility to another. Here's a fairly typical look at what happens and when to expect it:

4:30 A.M.	Wake-up call for people staying in motel
5:00 A.M.	Breakfast at motel
6:00 A.M.	Arrive at MEPS
6:30 A.M.	Official welcome
6:45 A.M.	Fill out medical histories
7:30 A.M.	Aptitude tests
10:30 A.M.	Medical screening
Noon	Lunch
1 P.M.	Meet with job counselor

3 P.M.   Meet for pre-enlistment interview

4 P.M.   Take oath of enlistment.

The medical screening (10:30 A.M.) consists of some nonstrenuous exercises that help military doctors detect people who have problems affecting their strength and agility. Blood is drawn, urine samples are collected, blood pressure is checked, and vital signs are recorded. Everyone also sits down with a doctor for a personal discussion of medical histories.

When future military folks meet at the MEPS with the job counselor (1 P.M.), that's when they learn the results of their ASVAB tests. That's also the time when they find out which military training they'll be allowed to take and which military career fields they may be able to enter.

The preenlistment interview (3 P.M.) is another one-on-one discussion. This time, the subject is you. What is your understanding of the promises made by your recruiter? Have you been honest in all the paperwork you've filled out? Have you been truthful about your run-ins with the law, about drug and alcohol use? The preenlistment interview is the time to come clean. It will also include a fingerprinting; the fingerprints will be sent to FBI headquarters.

For most future recruits, the oath of enlistment (4 P.M.) puts them legally into the Delayed Entry Program, or DEP. This is the case even for those who plan to leave for boot camp in a few days. First, they go into the DEP; three or four days later, if there are no problems with their criminal checks and blood work, they'll come back a second time to the MEPS to take the oath of enlistment again. It's this second oath that legally puts someone into the military.

Any military officer can administer an enlistment oath. Many recruits want to have a father, mother, brother, sister, or friend give them the oath. Again, that's possible so long as the ceremony is at the MEPS and the person is a commissioned officer, either active-duty, reserve, or even retired. MEPS officials recommend those personalized oaths be administered during the second visit to the MEPS, since it's not always possible

---------- ★ ----------

"How did you get in the Navy? How did you get on our side?"

—Lt. (j.g.) Roberts (Henry Fonda) in *Mister Roberts*
(Warner Brothers, 1955)

to estimate within a couple hours when a group will reach that point in their processing.

THE OATH OF ENLISTMENT

Everyone who joins the military takes the same oath. It's a solemn statement of the highest ideals of military service. Many veterans get a chill up their spines just reading the words. Here is the oath that is administered at the MEPS, marking the formal legal transition from civilian to soldier, sailor, airman, Marine or Coast Guardsman:

I do solemnly swear that I will support and defend the Constitution of the United States against all enemies, foreign and domestic. That I will bear true faith and allegiance to the same. That I will obey the orders of the president of the United States and the orders of the officers appointed over me, according to regulations and the Uniform Code of Military Justice. So help me God.

★ ★ 9 ★ ★

GETTING READY FOR BOOT CAMP

You've weighed the pros and cons. You've studied the incentives, training, and assignments offered by the services. You've picked the brains of family members, friends, and schoolmates who've been on active duty recently. You've made your decision, and you've signed on the dotted line. Now what?

The interval between the time you legally become a member of the armed forces by taking that oath at the MEPS center and the time you step onto the bus bound for boot camp can be a few days or as much as a year. Regardless of the length (and you'll know from your recruiter how long it will be for you), there are some things to do in advance to ease the transition from civilian to soldier.

The single most important thing to do is pay attention to the paperwork that the military sends every recruit before he or she leaves home for boot camp. That material contains guidance that can be surprisingly detailed, to include the kinds of underwear you can—and cannot—bring. Pay attention to it, and don't even daydream about sneaking something onto base that the military doesn't want to see.

What follows here is some general advice that might not be included in the paperwork you receive before boot camp, along with some information that will give you an idea of what to expect.

THE PHYSICAL FACTOR

The military is a physically demanding job, and at boot camp drill instructors give recruits a strenuous workout to see if they're capable of withstanding the rigors of active duty, and also to build their stamina and physical strength.

The physical conditioning in boot camp is geared to start with an average American teenager. Few recruits are Olympic-class athletes or weight lifters. Most recruits are pretty average, and that's the point at which the physical fitness aspect of boot camp begins.

Still, it's a good idea for anyone planning to attend boot camp to begin a personal conditioning program in advance. Three elements—running, push-ups and sit-ups—are all it takes. Try running for thirty minutes every other day. Unless you were a serious track-and-field athlete, don't think about running longer. But time your runs and see if you can't increase the distance you cover in those thirty minutes. It's the same thing with push-ups and sit-ups: stop when you've done as many as you can comfortably achieve. For sit-ups, remember to bend your knees. The goal for all physical conditioning is to make you stronger over time—which means it will take time to see results.

Reality Check: It would be nice to go to boot camp a little stronger and with more stamina. But it would be really dumb to show up with an injury that could have been prevented if you'd been realistic about your conditioning program. Those things can wash a recruit out of boot camp on the first day. Don't overdo it.

A couple of other issues have a bearing on your physical conditioning—smoking and alcohol. Boot camp is a no-tobacco, no-drinking environment. Period. That includes on your own time, and even off base. People who enter boot camp as smokers face the tough challenge of becoming nonsmokers and soldiers at the same time. Based on the experiences of people who've been there and done that, it's safe to say it's far easier to kick the smoking habit before reporting for the first day of training. Dippers, chewers, snuffers, and other practitioners of the tobacco habit are in the same boat. It's not enough to go smokeless; drill instructors expect their trainees to be tobaccoless.

The same rule applies to people with the alcohol habit. Alcoholism doesn't afflict only elderly men who sleep on sidewalks. Anyone can become an alcoholic, at any age. Women, due to the way their bodies process alcohol, are especially vulnerable to becoming alcoholics at a young age, after only a few years of active drinking. Unfortunately, there isn't any test to detect alcoholism.

Here's one useful rule of thumb: You may be an alcoholic if you consistently end up drinking more than you planned to. If you can't imagine how you'll go through boot camp without a drink—especially, if that idea frightens you—maybe it's time to confront the issue. Check the local tele-

———————— ☆ ————————

"You will go to the Degobah system. There you will learn from Yoda,
the Jedi master, who instructed me."

—Obi-wan Kenobi (Alec Guinness) to Luke Skywalker
(Mark Hamill) in *Star Wars: The Empire Strikes Back*
(Twentieth Century Fox, 1980)

———————————————

phone book for Alcoholics Anonymous. Call and find out the time and place of a meeting. Go to the meeting (they typically last one hour), listen (nobody will hassle or embarrass you), and decide if you've got a problem (you're the only one who can make that decision). The good news is that if you are in fact an alcoholic, Alcoholics Anonymous has more than sixty years of experience helping people face situations that make boot camp look like a summer picnic.

If you suspect you're a drug addict (as opposed to someone who's experimented with drugs a few times), don't even start down the road that leads to a military uniform. In all probability, you'll find yourself with a drug problem, plus some serious legal troubles, courtesy of the U.S. armed forces.

THE MEDICAL FACTOR

The military provides free medical care for everyone in uniform. There are no charges for doctor's visits, hospitalization, medicine, rehabilitation, or anything else needed for good health care. Those benefits are available to everyone from the first day they step into boot camp. A couple of tips, however, might smooth away rough spots:

Glasses

If you wear prescription eyeglasses, bring a written prescription. Your eye doctor can write it out, and so can the place where you bought your glasses. Keep the prescription in your wallet until you're settled into boot camp. Don't be surprised if your drill instructor doesn't let you wear prescription sunglasses.

Medicine

The military has an official "zero tolerance" policy for illegal drugs. When confronted with something that might be illegal drugs, they get really tough. If you bring any prescription medicine to boot camp, bring the doctor's written prescription too. If you bring nonprescription medicine, like hay fever medicine or even aspirin, try to bring an unopened bottle or box; recruits have been known to smuggle illegal drugs inside such containers. Be prepared to have your drill sergeant throw it away and order you to buy new medicine on base. They're that tough about even the suggestion of illegal drugs.

THE FINANCIAL FACTOR

The days of recruits getting a wad of money on payday are long gone. The military now pays its people by transferring funds electronically into their private checking or savings accounts. That means that recruits are expected to show up at boot camp with their own checking or savings accounts.

Before leaving for active duty, stop by your bank and talk to one of the officials there about having the military transfer your pay electronically. Each bank has an identifying code, usually a nine-digit number, which is also printed on the bottom of each check. You'll need to be able to give that number to finance officials when you report to boot camp, along with a second code number for your specific checking or savings account.

Don't worry about cashing out-of-state checks at boot camp. It happens all the time. Besides, you won't have much opportunity—or need—for it.

A financial problem that some recruits have to anticipate involves long-standing debts, like car loans and credit cards. Don't count on those bills getting forwarded to you in boot camp and finding you on time. Among the options that recruits have used:

- Go to boot camp debt free.
- Arrange for a family member to get the bills and pay them.
- Arrange for a family member to get the bills and forward them to you.
- See if you can delay payment for two or three months.

People who are entering the military with others financially dependent upon them—like spouses, children, even parents and siblings—should try to build up a financial cushion. Mixups tend to happen at the worst possible times.

THE FAMILY FACTOR

In one sense, boot camps are isolated places. The military wants the full attention of the men and women who are learning to become members of the armed forces. "Visitor hours" at boot camp come on graduation day; telephone calls relayed to recruits are limited to genuine emergencies; and the opportunities for recruits to make telephone calls are spotty.

Folks with a spouse or a child should expect to be cut off from their loved ones for the duration of boot camp. Family members of recruits aren't eligible for government-paid moves to boot camp, nor can they live in on-base housing. The most trusted means of communication is the old-fashioned way, writing letters.

Fortunately, it's easy for people in boot camp to meet their financial obligations to their families. There can't be any problems if the government is depositing each paycheck electronically into a savings or checking account to which a spouse or other family member has access.

THE EMOTIONAL FACTOR

What would you guess is the problem that recruits and drill instructors consistently identify as the biggest, roughest obstacle in boot camp? It's homesickness.

More people want to leave boot camp because they miss their friends and family than are driven out because they can't take the physical challenges of training.

For most people, boot camp is the longest period that they've ever been separated from the friendly, familiar feel of home, and the old neighborhood. It's also a dividing line in their lives, separating life as they have known it from life as it's going to be. Boot camp makes it clear, in a way that high school graduation or the first job does not, that you're an adult now. Everything is going to be different, and there's no turning back.

The key to overcoming any obstacle is recognizing it. Even if you consider yourself a hard-nosed, unsentimental character, expect homesickness to rear up suddenly at boot camp and hit you with a wallop that takes your breath away. It's part of the boot camp experience; it doesn't mean that you're weak.

———— ✬ ————

"We're not violent people. This is our first gun."

—Ellen Griswald (Beverly D'Angelo) in
National Lampoon's Vacation (Warner Brothers, 1983)

While you cannot completely prevent it, there are a couple things you can do to minimize it.

First, before you leave, ask some family members and friends to write you at boot camp. Don't be shy. Don't be vague. Make a direct request, and get a clear commitment. Then make sure your parents or spouse knows who's on your personal support network. One of the first things everyone does at boot camp is fill out a postcard notifying their families that they've arrived and giving the exact mailing address.

Second, make an effort to build a second support network among your fellow trainees. Some of this happens naturally, but really put yourself out to talk to other recruits. Trust your "gut feelings." Some of your fellow recruits will be people you're naturally drawn to, and some will be people you don't like. Recognize that if the idea of talking to strangers sounds impossible, you're exactly the kind of person who needs that support network the most. Don't stop when you get a "best friend" but continue until you discover that there are several people around you who can be counted on in various ways.

PACKING FOR BOOT CAMP

Generally, recruits shouldn't bring more than two suitcases. Keep in mind that you may end up carrying your suitcases for some distance; lighter is better. Since the military is supplying your clothes, there isn't much you have to bring.

To give you a sense of the kinds of things on the "Do Bring," "Don't Bring," and "Don't Even Think about Bringing" lists, here are some sample items:

Do Bring:
- Underwear (they'll tell you how much)
- Writing materials
- Religious materials
- Good jogging shoes
- Cheap wrist watch (with a light)
- Checkbook, account information
- Prescription medicine
- Copy of written prescriptions.

Don't Bring:
- Much civilian clothes (they'll tell you how much)
- CD or cassette players

- White socks with logos
- Much jewelry (one or two items are usually OK)
- Excessive makeup
- Cameras
- Computers.

Iffy:
- Transistor radios
- Small flashlights
- Nonreligious books
- Curlers for women
- Earrings for men
- Playing cards, dice
- Lighters.

Banned:
- Illegal drugs
- Alcohol
- Tobacco products
- Firearms
- Knives
- Pornography.

The list of "Iffy" items varies by service and sometimes by installation. Don't take it for granted that if a friend last year brought a couple paperback novels to boot camp, you'll be able to do the same this year.

10

BOOT CAMP BASICS

You've thought carefully about joining the military. You've researched its educational benefits and considered the way those programs fit into your own plans. You've looked at the training and assignments that you would receive and, again, weighed their impact upon your own near-term and long-term career goals. You've made a realistic appraisal of the way you would react to being separated from your family and friends, and you know that you're going to have to construct a family-away-from-the-family once you're in uniform.

There's only one obstacle remaining—boot camp!

Borrowing the physical tests of the Spanish Inquisition, the mental ordeals of a few nights on Elm Street, and the personal touch of an insane asylum run by the patients, boot camp is supposed to be one place in our society where systematic abuse of people is condoned, all in the name of separating the men from the boys, the women from the girls, the soldiers from the civilians, and everyone from their own sense of self-respect.

At least, that's the way that the military's introductory training course—known officially by many names but most commonly called, simply, boot camp—has been portrayed throughout the decades in countless books and, especially, in the movies.

The truth is quite different. More than two-hundred thousand people go through boot camp every year. It's demanding but not sadistic. The vast majority of people consider it a positive experience in their lives. The toughness is reasonable, and the purpose is clearly to get people to see that they're capable of more than they ever thought possible—physically, emotionally, and yes, even mentally.

As we've done a few times already, let's start our look at this strange, new, military institution by seeing it through the eyes of someone who has been there.

MARTIN'S STORY: TOUGH WORK AND CARING

Eight years after finishing boot camp, Martin Celestine still has a clear image of his drill sergeant.

"His uniform was always clean, regardless what we'd just done. When we ran, he ran faster. It seemed like he was the fittest man in the world."

For the last year and a half, Celestine, a veteran of peacekeeping operations in Macedonia and Hungary, has thought a lot about his drill sergeant. For he has become one himself—a member of a unique band of men and women responsible for guiding the newest members of the U.S. military through their first couple months in uniform.

Each of the services has some of its top enlisted members work directly with the troops during basic training, as boot camp is more formally known.

Usually, they are volunteers. They must pass a screening process, followed by intensive training. Marches, physical fitness drills, marksmanship tests, and classroom exams are part of the process of becoming a drill instructor.

"Before you can instruct your soldiers about a marching movement, you have to know the movement yourself. And you have to be able to articulate it," Celestine said.

An Army staff sergeant (E-6) and a native of the Virgin Islands, Celestine volunteered to become a drill sergeant. It's considered one of the toughest assignments in the military today. The men and women who successfully handle the job get faster promotions and better assignments.

Those kinds of personal payoffs are in the future for most drill sergeants. The downside to the job can be considerable. Although they get a

———— ★ ————

"Maybe it's just me, but I think our little adventures
lately are getting stupid."

—Mitch Robbins (Billy Crystal) in *City Slickers*
(MGM, 1991)

monthly bonus of $275, many see extra expenses eat away at that income. Family life suffers. Being a drill sergeant is not a nine-to-five job.

"During the first two weeks of basic training, we're there from 4 o'clock in the morning to 9 o'clock at night. I'll just sleep in the office."

Like many drill instructors, Celestine isn't happy with the way Hollywood depicts people in his job. Belittling people, swearing at recruits, hitting soldiers, or encouraging recruits to haze others—all are high on the list of things that aren't done.

"The stress is supposed to be between the soldier and the task, not between the soldier and the drill sergeant," he said.

In the Army, Navy, Air Force and Coast Guard, drill instructors build military values upon the values that each recruit brings into the service. The Marine Corps leads its recruits down a tougher path during its boot camp.

But Celestine doesn't think that the Army's basic training is necessarily easier today than it's been in the past. "With all the technology we teach today, basic training is very demanding. It's more than push-ups, sit-ups and screaming. There is a lot of emphasis upon academics."

There's also a lot of emphasis on growing up and learning about values. That was one of many lessons that Celestine learned years ago from his drill sergeant.

"He never laughed with us. But you knew he cared."

WHAT MAKES BOOT CAMP TICK?

One of the most important things for recruits to understand before their first day in uniform is that boot camp is perhaps the most meticulously planned event that they will ever participate in. Nothing happens there by chance. Everything has been studied, quantified, charted, challenged, and defended. What is done, how it's done, why it should be done, and how it is communicated to recruits are among the most examined interactions between human beings on this planet. Constant examination of boot camp has been going on for decades, it's going on now, and one can reasonably predict it will happen for as long as people dress in distinctive clothing, walk in step, and salute each other.

Hollywood may portray boot camp as a place where angry men have the government's permission to mistreat people. Not so. Tough talk and raised voices may be common, but even those outbursts are coldly calculated.

Boot camp is the place where new members of the military learn the rules. Some of that information is factual—how to tell one rank from another, how to fire a rifle, how to treat some basic injuries. But the part of

———————— ☆ ————————

"You burr-headed idiots do not appreciate my gentle 'good morning.'
When my back is turned, you call me bad names."

—Tech. Sgt. Jim Moore (Jack Webb) in *The DI*
(Warner Brothers, 1957)

———————————————

boot camp that people remember has more to do with the culture of the military—the insistence upon obedience, the critical eye looking at the smallest detail, the emphasis upon teamwork.

In the grand scheme of things, it doesn't matter whether your toothbrush is to the left or the right of the comb that you might store in a footlocker. But it is crucial to the military—and to the lives of everyone around you in the military, and ultimately to the security of the nation—that people in uniform perform exactly as they've been ordered. In boot camp, the placement of a toothbrush will become of monumental importance, because it's one step in a recruit's education in obedience and another test of his or her ability to pay attention to details.

Since physical conditioning is important to the military, it is an important part of boot camp. Just remember that tens of millions of Americans have gone through boot camp, and nearly two-hundred thousand will experience it the same year that you attend. You don't have to be Arnold Schwarzenegger to survive.

WHERE AND WHEN

Because of the special nature of the training, boot camps are only offered at a small number of military installations. The duration of the training also varies.

Here are the lengths of boot camp and the locations it was offered at the turn of the twenty-first century:

Army: Nine weeks at Fort Benning, Georgia (near Columbus); Fort Jackson, South Carolina (in Columbia); Fort Knox, Kentucky (thirty-five miles south of Louisville); Fort Leonard Wood, Missouri (in St. Robert, 130 miles south of St. Louis); or Fort Sill, Oklahoma (near Lawton).

Navy: Nine weeks at the Great Lakes Naval Training Center, Illinois (about forty miles north of Chicago).

Air Force: Six weeks at Lackland Air Force Base, Texas (ten miles south of San Antonio).

Marines: Twelve weeks at Parris Island Recruit Depot, South Carolina (forty miles north of Savannah); or San Diego Recruit Depot, California.

Coast Guard: Eight weeks at Cape May Training Center, New Jersey (fifty miles south of Atlantic City).

Keep in mind, that boot camp is only the start of military training. The vast majority of recruits go from boot camp, where they learn the basics about military life, to a second training course where they learn the specific job-related skills that they'll be using every day that they're in uniform. That second, skills-oriented training may be at the same installation as boot camp, or it may be somewhere else.

The Army has a program for certain people in which boot camp and that skills-related training are rolled into one course, called "One-Station Unit Training" or OSUT (pronounced "oh-sut"). New sailors and Coast Guardsmen can go directly to the fleet after boot camp. That lets them see the practical side of the various jobs before actually picking one.

THE BIG PICTURE

As we've seen, everyone who joins one of the armed forces as an enlisted person goes through boot camp. Officers don't go to boot camp, but they have their own training courses that do many of the same things. People going directly into the reserves and National Guard must attend full-time boot camp; they can't go through it one weekend at a time.

The people who actually work with recruits are a special group of men and women. Each training unit will have its own drill instructors, usually three men and women. Those same drill instructors will follow the recruits throughout each minute of boot camp. The same drill instructors will wake their recruits up in the morning and turn off the lights at night.

We're calling them "drill instructors" for simplicity's sake, but each branch of the military has its own title. Here's the breakdown:

Army: drill sergeant

Navy: recruit division commander (RDC)

Air Force: military training instructor (MTI)

Marines: drill instructor (DI)

Coast Guard: company commander (CC)

Once boot camp begins, recruits are in a highly controlled environment. They cannot leave the training camp, nor can they receive visitors. Opportunities to make a telephone call are limited, and only in genuine emergencies can outsiders reach recruits on the telephone; even then it's difficult and requires the help of drill instructors.

The military exerts more control over the time of recruits than anything they've ever experienced before. From the time they get up in the morning until the time they go to sleep at night, new members of the military discover that their drill instructors decide what they do, how they do it, when they do it, and how long they'll do it.

Everyone in boot camp eats, sleeps, exercises, trains, studies, and relaxes as a member of a unit. Very little is done individually. Very little opportunity exists to meet people from other units. Unless something goes wrong, each recruit will remain with the same unit throughout boot camp. About the only situation in which a recruit would leave the unit is when a medical problem makes him or her unable to continue with the training regime. In those instances, recruits start again—from the very beginning—with a new training unit.

Many of the controls over recruits loosen gradually during the length of boot camp. Like everything that happens there, this is a highly planned process. The purpose is to let recruits feel that they are being rewarded for the good job they are doing.

Something to Remember: The most stressful day of boot camp for most people is the day they arrive. That's based on studies done by the military. The second-most stressful is the second day, and so on.

IF THINGS GO WRONG

Boot camp is a highly structured, highly planned activity. It's not a place of random brutality. There are limits to everything. Even the rawest recruit doesn't have to endure certain things.

- Drill instructors can be tough, but they can't hit.
- Drill instructors can raise their voices, but they can't use slurs that are racial, sexist, religious or ethnic.
- Drill instructors cannot have sexual relations with the people they're training, even if it's consensual.

If a recruit is asked to do something that he feels he cannot safely do—whether it's climbing a rope or walking for miles in the hot sun—there is always the option of not doing it. Don't expect the drill instructor to take the news that you don't want to march anymore with calm acceptance. Getting pushed to the limits of human endurance is one of the things that people are supposed to experience in boot camp. Still, declining to go any

———————— ★ ————————

"You hang around with nice people, you get nice friends."
—Rocky Balboa (Sylvester Stallone) in *Rocky*
(MGM, 1976)

farther is always an option. There may be consequences, ranging from extra work to dismissal from the military, but stopping or refusing to do something is always a possibility.

Trainees should be free of sexual pressure from other trainees. Everyone's private life is their personal business, including the off-duty, off-base lives of homosexuals and lesbians. But just as no one has to endure activity from the opposite sex that makes them uncomfortable, they don't have to let someone of their own gender make them uncomfortable. Gays and lesbians are supposed to be free from harassment from other trainees.

Many routes are open to trainees who feel that drill instructors or other trainees have crossed the line. The military always prefers that people start with their own supervisors, but when the supervisor is the problem, there are other options. Military lawyers and investigators known as "inspectors general" are another route for complaints. Chaplains can either help directly or advise recruits how to proceed with getting a problem resolved.

Author's Note: One of the toughest things about boot camp for me was waking up at five o'clock in the morning, knowing that I'd be awake until ten that night, and also knowing that the only decision I would make between those two events was when I went to the bathroom.

Lack of control is a frightening experience. The toughest parent or the worst boss doesn't control your life as completely as a typical drill instructor. Things are worse if you start thinking, as I caught myself doing, that such lack of control would last throughout my time in the military.

But that's not the case. The military isn't that different from the civilian world. In fact, the amount of control recruits get over their own lives increases throughout boot camp. Being someone who makes a living in a military uniform is closer to the civilian world than it is to boot camp.

11

BOOT CAMP DETAILS

One of the nice things about boot camp—and basic training is a place where it's important to find nice things—is that no one has to worry about figuring out what to do. Nor must anyone bone up in advance about what to expect. Drill instructors will tell each recruit exactly what to do, how to do it, and when to do it. Boot camp is a zero-uncertainty zone.

In fact, there are some drawbacks to going into boot camp with too much detailed information. Basic training is in constant flux. Many installations, and even the individual training units upon the same base, may differ from each other in minor details that assume huge importance in the life of any recruit. What's the exact layout of a room at boot camp? What belongings go where? When's breakfast?

All those answers, and many more, will be revealed without a single recruit ever having to ask. Everyone can count on the answers coming from a drill instructor to be accurate.

Still, it can be helpful to get an idea in advance what to expect. That's the purpose of this chapter. Keep in mind that the information that follows is based on generalizations. The rules and procedures in any specific boot camp can be quite different.

WHERE YOU LIVE

Everyone at boot camp is assigned to a specific training unit. Each unit has its own living quarters. That may be in a single large room where several dozen beds line a central walkway, or it could be college-like dormitory shared by four or more people. Single rooms are unheard of.

Married recruits cannot live with their families during boot camp. In fact, the families of people in boot camp are ineligible for on-base military housing. It's unlikely that married recruits will be able to see their families until one of the last weekends of boot camp.

The movement of recruits is severely restricted. Only in the last weeks of boot camp are they permitted to leave the immediate area of their barracks or dormitories during their private time. That's no big deal, because recruits don't have any private time for the first weeks of basic training.

Drill instructors may let recruits pick their own beds on the first day, or they may assign people to beds. Once that decision is made, it's locked in. Unless something extraordinary happens, that's where everyone stays for the duration of boot camp. Not getting along with one's neighbors isn't a good reason to be assigned to another bed.

Whether "home" is a single barracks' room with fifty other people or a dormitory with three roommates, one thing can be counted on. There will be rules involving every single thing in the room—from combs and toothbrushes to uniforms, boots, and towels. The rules will say where each item will go.

The bed and the area immediately around it take on huge importance in boot camp. Each recruit is responsible for making his or her own bed to exacting specifications. Typically, each recruit also is responsible for a footlocker and a wall locker, in which are stored the uniforms that recruits get during the first day of boot camp. A small area may be set aside in each wall locker and footlocker for personal property, but there are also rules about where those areas are and what they can contain.

That small area of physical space under a recruit's control will be the focus of much of the drill instructor's most basic lessons in military life. Can recruits take directions? Will they show a sense of responsibility, even pride, in the things for which they are responsible? Are they capable of giving their full attention to little tasks? If they are put under pressure for

---

★

"Out on that drill field yesterday you people were miserable.
You people ain't even a mob. . . . You clowns are a herd.
I'm going to get me a sheepdog. I've seen better
maneuvering in a Chinese fire-drill."

—Tech. Sgt. Jim Moore (Jack Webb) in *The DI*
(Warner Brothers, 1957)

———— ☆ ————

"God didn't make Rambo. I made him."

—Col. Samuel Trautman (Richard Crenna) in
First Blood (Artisan Entertainment, 1982)

———————————

minor infractions, can they take it like adults? Are they capable of learning from mistakes and improving?

Recruits are also responsible for maintaining certain common areas— from the hallways and latrines of their barracks or dormitories to the grounds immediately around those buildings. Here again, things are often more than they seem. For in maintaining these larger areas, drill instructors are both testing and teaching. Can the recruits work as a team? Do they take responsibility for each other? Can they find ways of resolving—or suppressing—conflicts between each other while they work on a common task?

TYPICAL DAY

Every hour of every day at boot camp is planned, and no two days are exactly alike. To give you an idea what a day may look like, let's select July 14, 1999, at the Air Force's boot camp:

4:55 A.M.	Reveille
5:00 A.M.	Physical conditioning
6:30 A.M.	Breakfast
7:00 A.M.	Preparing for dorm inspection
8:00 A.M.	Practice marching
10:00 A.M.	Instruction in GI Bill
11:00 A.M.	Drill instructor's lessons
11:30 A.M.	Lunch
12:30 P.M.	Get on buses
1:00 P.M.	Instruction on career fields
5:00 P.M.	Back on buses
5:30 P.M.	Dinner
6:30 P.M.	Briefing
9:00 P.M.	Lights out

Note that everything is done as a member of a group. There are no "electives," no accelerated courses, and no individual study. Also notice that on this particular day, the unit goes to another location for training in the afternoon. All other activities of that day revolve upon the unit's dormitory, which means the unit drill instructors are the ones performing the training.

On most nights, after the final activity of the day, there is a brief period—thirty minutes to a couple of hours—for study, preparing uniforms for the next day, perhaps even writing a letter. There's no time for television, and most recruits won't even get the chance to go to the movie theater until one of their final weekends at boot camp.

TWO IMPORTANT DECISIONS

Boot camp isn't a time for making decisions. Mostly, it's about learning to hear—really hear—instructions and to carry out orders with precision, neither "reading" things into them nor falling short. But all recruits do make two decisions during the first weeks of boot camp that have a profound impact upon them and their families.

Montgomery GI Bill

The GI Bill has been around since World War II. Under the rules for the current version, called the Montgomery GI Bill, new service members have a one-time chance to take part. That opportunity comes during the first weeks of boot camp. Folks who turn it down will not be given a chance later to change their minds and sign up.

Those with families may find it a difficult decision, because unlike earlier versions of the GI Bill, the Montgomery GI Bill requires participants to approve a deduction from their pay for a year. That deduction is a hundred dollars a month—no more, no less—and it lasts for the first twelve months in uniform. No one can decide to have the money come from a later twelve-month period.

In return, for every dollar a new military member has deducted, the government contributes at least fifteen dollars that can be used to pay tuition, books, and fees. Some military members receive more, under a program of "kickers" that are part of the incentives offered by a recruiter.

Author's Advice: Take it. No other investment guarantees at least fifteen dollars for each dollar you contribute. Even with the deduction, most folks are able to build nice savings accounts during their first year in uniform, because the government pays so many living expenses.

Life Insurance

Another one-time decision that recruits make during the first weeks of boot camp involves the government-backed life insurance. It's called Servicemember's Group Life Insurance (SGLI), and it costs sixteen dollars per month to receive the maximum coverage of two hundred thousand dollars. That means that if someone dies in the military, the person or people whom the service member designated will receive two hundred thousand dollars. It makes no difference whether the death is military related, caused by disease, results from a car accident, or comes from any other cause.

The process of getting involved with SGLI is the reverse of the process for the Montgomery GI Bill. Everyone is automatically covered by SGLI from the moment they come on active duty, and sixteen dollars are automatically taken from their monthly paychecks. Recruits must take action to *stop* SGLI. They can also decide to provide something less than two-hundred thousand dollars in coverage to their survivors.

Author's Advice: Take this, too. Everyone is automatically covered by SGLI because it's that good a deal. There's no way that commercial life insurance comes close to this policy. No one with a family can afford to pass it up. Even single people should go ahead, because it can make a huge difference in the lives of your parents, brothers, or sisters. Sixteen dollars is less than two movie tickets a month. Do it!

PAY AND BENEFITS

People in boot camp might feel like they haven't yet been truly admitted into the military, but in the eyes of the law they're as much active-duty members as the grizzled veteran with a couple decades in uniform. The full range of military benefits is available to them and, with a few major exceptions, to the members of their families.

In fact, eligibility for military pay starts the moment folks raise their hands and take the oath of enlistment. That usually happens at the MEPS

---- ☆ ----

"Let's do the grab-the-rifle-by-the-bottom thing."

—Sgt. Bilko (Steve Martin) in *Sgt. Bilko*
(Universal Studios, 1996)

center. So, it's not unusual for people to be owed a few days of pay by the military before they step foot onto their basic training camp.

Remember that most people actually take two formal oaths. The first puts them into the Delayed Entry Program (DEP), and the second is the enlistment oath. The DEP oath doesn't establish any rights for pay.

Pay Day

Regardless when the clock begins ticking for pay, the first paycheck won't come until boot camp.

Payday in the military comes twice a month—on the fifteenth and at the end of the month. It's possible for recruits to receive an emergency payment upon arrival at basic training, but they won't get it just by asking. They'll have to justify the payment to their drill instructor and, probably, to others as well.

Debit Cards

Increasingly, boot camps give new-arrivals "debit cards." They look and work like credit cards. The magnetic strip on the back of the card records that a recruit is credited with having a certain amount of money—usually around two hundred dollars. Each new purchase is electronically subtracted from that amount. The value of the debit card is subtracted from the first paycheck. If you get a debit card at boot camp, listen closely when the rules are explained. They might be honored only by on-base stores, not by civilian shops outside the main gate.

Amounts

The salary (called "Basic Pay") for recruits in the year 2000 was $930 monthly. From that are subtracted taxes, Montgomery GI Bill withholdings and SGLI premiums.

People with families—spouses, children, or parents with no income—can receive several hundred dollars more each month. That extra money comes from two different sources. One is called the Family Separation Allowance. For those in boot camp and the follow-up on skill-related courses, it's a flat rate of $100 monthly.

A second, separate payment, called the Basic Housing Allowance (BHA), was designed to help meet the housing costs of the family. Rates are based upon two factors—the service member's rank and the place the family lives. Amounts for recruits can be a few dollars or a few hundred dollars.

Freebies

During boot camp and follow-up on skill-related training, the military provides food and shelter. There's no cost to recruits for these benefits. Recruits receive the full amount of their Basic Pay. Nor is there any charge for their uniforms, their equipment, training materials, or government-provided transportation.

Nor are they billed for any health-care-related services, from visits to the doctor to major surgery, from prescription medicine to prescription eye-glasses, from dental services to any other medical procedure.

Other Benefits

Recruits receive military identification cards (ID cards) that give them access to government-subsidized stores that operate on most installations. At boot camp, there will be military department stores (called "exchanges"), food stores (called "commissaries"), or the military's version of the convenience store, which goes by many names.

Family Benefits

Spouses of people on active duty also qualify for military ID cards and become eligible to shop at any on-base military store. That right isn't confined to the place where boot camp is being held, or even to an installation of the same branch of the armed forces.

Spouses and children also qualify for health-care coverage from the military. Medical care for family members is provided by one of the military's health-insurance programs, CHAMPUS and TriCare. Both programs may require family members to pay certain fees for visiting civilian doctors and hospitals.

Spouses and children can receive dental care from military dentists if space is available, which it often isn't. Many military families purchase government-backed dental insurance policies costing eighteen to twenty dollars monthly.

The fact that the military will not pay to move family members to the vicinity of boot camp, nor will it allow them to move into on-base housing,

———— ☆ ————

Boot camp is a zero-uncertainty zone.

isn't the same thing as saying a spouse cannot move to a community near boot camp. People can do that. But the military tightly controls the time of people in basic training. Odds are that a boot camp participant might only see a spouse a couple times, for an hour or two.

Important Hair-Splitting: The military's benefits for family members are for spouses. A spouse is someone with a marriage certificate. Girlfriends and boyfriends aren't eligible for any military benefits, even if they're fully dependent upon someone now in uniform for their financial support.

Parents can qualify for many of the benefits that go to the families of military people, but it's tough to make that happen. The parents must receive more than half of their income from the military member, and they may be required to prove that they actually lived before boot camp in a home provided by the military member.

★ ★ 12 ★ ★

SURVIVAL KIT OF INFORMATION

Everything that everyone needs to know about boot camp will be given to them when the military expects them to know it. The "cramming" that many of us did at school before an important examination isn't necessary. Still, it's nice to know a few things in advance.

What follows in this chapter are some useful nuggets of information that everyone is expected to master by the time they leave basic training. For some items, refer to the appendices in the back of the book for more details, especially for things that can be depicted graphically.

RANK

Everyone in the military has stuff on their uniforms that tells the world exactly where they fit into the structure. This "stuff" can take the form of metallic devices on shirt collars or on the tops of shoulders, or colored cloth on the shoulders or sleeves of shirts and coats. We're talking, of course, about rank.

It doesn't take much time to become familiar with the names and insignia of a particular service. Charts with the rank insignia of each branch of the military appear in Appendix C of this book.

Each branch of the military has its own insignia for each rank and its own name for the rank. Sometimes, as we'll discuss later, the insignia and the name are used by more than one service.

But what happens when a navy lieutenant commander and an army captain have to work together (which is happening increasingly often today). Who's in charge?

There's a quick way to find out. Each rank has a letter of the alphabet and a number associated with it. That two-item code is called "a pay grade." Under this scheme, every enlisted person can be identified as an "E-something." For example, everyone starting at the lowest rung of the military ladder is an E-1. On their first promotion, every enlisted person gets a new rank (private, seaman apprentice, airman, or private first class, depending on service), but they also get a new pay grade. They become E-2s. There are nine pay grades for enlisted folks. So the most senior enlisted people in uniform are E-9s.

By using pay grades, you can figure out who is your equal, your junior, and your senior in another service.

Officer pay grades start with the letter O. There are ten officer pay grades, from O-1 (second lieutenants and ensigns) to O-10 (four-star generals and four-star admirals). Between the officer and the enlisted scales is a group of people known as "warrant officers." Their pay grade starts with a W, and there are four or five levels, depending on the service.

When two people of equal rank are working together, the one who has been in that rank longer is senior. Military folks talk about "date of rank," the day they assumed a rank.

Answer: At the beginning of this section, the question was asked about the Navy lieutenant commander and the Army captain. Which was senior? The lieutenant commander. In the Navy and Coast Guard, lieutenant commanders are O-4s, while captains in the Army, Air Force and Marine Corps are O-3s.

TIME

In the military, time is reckoned using a twenty-four-hour clock. Supper isn't at 5 P.M.; it's at 1700 (spoken as "seventeen hundred"). Once you get the hang of it, it's very easy. Just add "1200" to every time between noon and midnight. Here's how that breaks down for the day:

Civilian Time	Military Time	Pronunciation
Midnight	2400	Twenty four hundred
1:00 A.M.	0100	Zero one hundred
2:00 A.M.	0200	Zero two hundred
3:00 A.M.	0300	Zero three hundred
4:00 A.M.	0400	Zero four hundred
5:00 A.M.	0500	Zero five hundred
6:00 A.M.	0600	Zero six hundred
7:00 A.M.	0700	Zero seven hundred
8:00 A.M.	0800	Zero eight hundred

9:00 A.M..	0900	Zero nine hundred
10:00 A.M.	1000	Ten hundred
11:00 A.M.	1100	Eleven hundred
Noon	1200	Twelve hundred
1:00 P.M.	1300	Thirteen hundred
2:00 P.M.	1400	Fourteen hundred
3:00 P.M.	1500	Fifteen hundred
4:00 P.M.	1600	Sixteen hundred
5:00 P.M.	1700	Seventeen hundred
6:00 P.M.	1800	Eighteen hundred
7:00 P.M.	1900	Nineteen hundred
8:00 P.M.	2000	Twenty hundred
9:00 P.M.	2100	Twenty-one hundred
10:00 P.M.	2200	Twenty-two hundred
11:00 P.M.	2300	Twenty-three hundred

Pronunciation of the minutes is very straightforward. Just say the numbers:

- 0001 (12:01 A.M.) is "zero zero zero one"
- 0215 (2:15 A.M.) is "zero two fifteen"
- 1545 (3:45 P.M.) is "fifteen forty-five"

While all of the military services keep time the same way under this twenty-four-hour clock, there is one peculiarity when it comes to talking about time. Ask a soldier or airman to convert 2:17 P.M. into military time, and he'll say "fourteen seventeen hours." A sailor, Marine or Coast Guardsman will just say "fourteen seventeen," leaving off the "hours."

ALPHABET

Anyone who has ever tried spelling the simplest word over the telephone knows what can happen. Telling someone the letters in "cat" can

---

★

"*Now*, according to my watch, does not mean *in the morning*."

—Lt. Cmdr. Queeg (Humphrey Bogart) in
The Caine Mutiny (Columbia Pictures, 1954)

take a very long time if the listener thinks the first letter is "g" or "d" or "e." The same sorts of misunderstandings can happen with the last letter of the word "cat."

The most important conversations that anyone in the military can have may be over a radio, with static crackling in the background, and some life-or-death issue hanging in the balance. To deal with just that kind of situation, the armed forces have developed something called "the phonetic alphabet." In this case, "phonetic" means "spoken." The phonetic alphabet is a way of spelling out words with the least chance of miscommunication.

In the phonetic alphabet, "charlie alpha tango" stands for "cat." One of the strengths of the phonetic alphabet is that the same word always stands for the same letter. "Cat" is never "chuckie apple tiger." Here's the complete phonetic alphabet:

A	alpha	B	bravo	C	charlie
D	delta	E	echo	F	foxtrot
G	golf	H	hotel	I	india
J	juliette	K	kilo	L	lima
M	mike	N	november	O	oscar
P	papa	Q	quebec	R	romeo
S	sierra	T	tango	U	uniform
V	victor	W	whiskey	X	x-ray
Y	yankee	Z	zulu		

PERSONAL CONDUCT

One of the major surprises that people unfamiliar with the military receive when they step into boot camp is the emphasis that all branches of the armed forces put upon values. Recruits may spend more time talking about personal integrity than firing at the rifle range.

"Can I buy a vowel?"

—Teacher Bill Rago (Danny DeVito) dealing with
military acronyms in *Renaissance Man*
(Touchstone Pictures, 1994)

Partly, that's because many kids don't receive that basic instruction when they're growing up. But mostly it's because the military doesn't fight as individuals but as units. If a unit is to hold together, everyone must know the basic rules of civility and fairness that let a collection of people work together.

Values are abstract, things like loyalty and honesty. There are also some issues dealing with personal conduct that the armed forces take a strong interest in, starting with the recruits at basic training.

Illegal Drugs

The military was the originator of the "zero tolerance" idea for drug abuse. Anyone bringing illegal drugs onto a military installation exposes himself to a world of hurt. Penalties for practically everything—use, possession, distribution—are much more severe in the military.

Drinking

Not too long ago, the military was tolerant of heavy drinking. No more. Recruits cannot bring any alcoholic beverage onto a military installation. They can be barred from consuming any alcohol while attending boot camp, even off base or in a private home. (Drill instructors will give the rules for each boot camp.)

Tobacco

The rules for tobacco products are similar to those for alcohol. Don't bring any into camp, and don't use any, even off base on your own time.

Theft

Stealing from another recruit is more than robbery; it's an attack against the trust that must exist in military units. Like illegal drug use, it's treated more harshly than in the civilian world.

Problems Off Base

In the civilian world, the boss doesn't worry about what employees do when they're not working. That's not true in the military. The services take an intense interest in everything affecting recruits, from off-duty fights to bad debts and legal troubles.

Sex

When you leave for boot camp, plan to be celibate until you graduate. There's no time or place for romantic encounters. As with alcohol, the military used to have a tolerant attitude toward prostitution. No more. In the era of AIDS, there's no such thing as a harmless fling.

The Marine Corps keeps a strict line between men and women at basic training. In boot camps run by the other services, men and women recruits may find themselves mixing together. Nothing can stop the natural chemistry between the sexes. But the military spells out severe consequences for anyone acting on those impulses. There's no such thing as consensual sex between a recruit and a trainer. Punishment can also come from consensual relations between two recruits at boot camp.

Harassment

Any attack upon a member of a unit is an attack upon the unit as a whole. Any recruit creating trouble for another person because of religion, race, ethnic background, or sexual orientation can expect the armed forces to come down hard.

Gays and Lesbians

The official policy of the military is to leave gay men and lesbians alone, so long as they don't make an issue of their orientation. Boot camp is the wrong place to figure out how much freedom a gay or lesbian can have in the military. During basic training, don't expect any latitude. Equal harshness will fall on the head of any recruit who takes it upon him or herself to "out" another recruit.

Reality Check: What we've been discussing may look like a long list of "thou shalt not's" that make boot camp a perilous place to be. Frankly, most people don't have any difficulty with any of these rules. Can you give up alcohol and tobacco while you're in training? Will you be able to avoid giving other recruits a bad time? Do you know the difference between the U.S. military and an escort service? If you can answer "Yes," to all of these questions, you can expect a smooth transition from the civilian world into life in a uniform.

SOME SIMPLE ADVICE

There's not much to do in advance of boot camp to learn to shoot a machine gun, clean and store a tent to military specifications, or drive a tank.

———— ☆ ————

"Maybe we, as officers, have a responsibility to this country to see that the men and women charged with its security are trained professionals. Yes, I'm sure I read that somewhere once."

—Col. Nathan Jessup (Jack Nicholson) in
A Few Good Men (Columbia Pictures, 1992)

But there's much that recruits can do to get their attitudes into proper condition. To a surprising degree, boot camp is about attitude. Here's some advice drawn from the experiences of boot camp survivors.

Listen

The single most important thing that people learn during basic training is about understanding instructions, doing what you're told, no more and no less, in such a way that the same instructions to you or someone else will result in the same thing being done the same way. Some folks find that very difficult to do. It all starts with listening, really listening, to what you're told.

Avoid Assumptions

Getting in the way of listening are the assumptions that flitter through our minds. If the drill instructor tells you to clean a trash can and you discover it's dirty because it's sitting next to a puddle on the side of a road, don't assume that the drill instructor just wants you to move the trash can.

In every war, lives are lost in combat because people make perfectly reasonable assumptions about what others want, what they intend to do, or where they intend to go. Another related lesson of boot camp is to get people to recognize when they're making an assumption. Instead of assuming, ask direct questions that will bring direct answers. Act on the information in the answers, not on your assumptions about someone's unspoken wishes.

Sweat the Little Things

Boot camp is about details, from learning the correct way to wear a uniform and march, to getting information about surviving in combat, and helping others to survive too. Boot camp is two or three months of learning one tiny piece of information after another.

One of the best ways to succeed at boot camp is to throw yourself into that strange world of details. Put your heart, mind, and soul into it. If you find yourself drying dishes, try to be the best dish-dryer the world has ever seen. Don't hold back.

Forget about Getting Even

Take a group of strangers, drop them in a pressure cooker, strip away all sense of privacy and the lives they've known, add long hours and physical exhaustion, remove their usual outlets for relieving stress, and toss in just a pinch of old-fashioned competition, and you've got a recipe for maximizing trouble between people.

Fantasies about straightening out some so-and-so are normal, even occasional daydreams about showing the drill instructor a thing or two some day. Don't dwell on those thoughts, and never act on them. One of the many purposes of boot camp is finding out how recruits react under stress. The ones who don't do well may find themselves losing out on assignments and training.

Courtesy

By the standards of the civilian world, the military's brand of protocol is pretty elaborate. A lot of it boils down to simple courtesy. "Please," "thank you," "excuse me," and "I'm sorry" can ease recruits past many problems with their drill instructors or even with other trainees.

Salutes

A military courtesy that doesn't have a civilian-world equal is the salute. Folks in uniform raise their right hands toward their heads under certain circumstances. At boot camp, recruits learn the way their service wants them to salute and about the times it's called for.

In every training unit, someone always gets bent out of shape because it seems the military is forcing them to respect people. No, the military is setting standards. According to those standards, everyone gives a salute under specific circumstances.

The salute is a greeting, a courtesy, an acknowledgment. It shouldn't be demeaning to say "Good morning" to someone you don't personally care for. Same for the salute.

Be Skeptical about Gossip

A not-so-honored military tradition involves new recruits talking about the good (or bad) deals they got from their recruiters and the ways they were helped (or lied to) by those folks. Don't let someone else's problems and bad information affect your attitude.

If you believe your recruiter withheld information or gave you bad information, check it out with your drill instructor. If there really is a problem, the drill instructor may be able to put you on the road to solving it. If you've gotten bad information from other recruits, they'll set you straight.

WINNING THE EMOTIONAL GAME

As we've already mentioned, the number-one problem at boot camp, according to drill instructors and graduates who are honest about the experience, isn't poor physical conditioning, weak academic skills, or difficulties accepting military-style discipline, but homesickness.

That shouldn't be surprising. Most people who enter basic training find themselves separated for the first time from their families, friends, neighborhoods and old routines. That's tough, that's difficult. It's a major upheaval that leads to all sorts of bad feelings that won't go away just by telling oneself that you're supposed to be "a big boy" or "a big girl" now.

All lives are lived in a particular setting, and boot camp signals for most recruits not only their entry into the military but their exit from childhood. There's no escaping that milestone. Getting it behind you is difficult.

The people who don't recognize and deal with their homesickness often have problems that show up in other ways. Their mental turmoil prevents them from getting enough rest, and suddenly they have problems with physical fitness tests that used to be a breeze; their performance in academic courses slips, because they're too groggy to be sharp. Or they may try to show they're not really scared by drinking too much when they have

———— ☆ ————

"R2D2, what are we doing here?"

—Luke Skywalker (Mark Hamill) arriving at the Jedi training planet in *Star Wars: The Empire Strikes Back* (Twentieth Century Fox, 1980)

the chance or taking risks in the field. Most commonly, they will convert their fear into anger that gets directed at the people around them.

To succeed at boot camp, you have to win "the emotional game" of basic training. That may entail doing some things—like going out of your way to talk to a stranger—that frighten you more than having a six-foot-four drill instructor screaming in your face.

Fortunately, from the experiences of hundreds of thousands of people who've gone through boot camp, we can learn dozens of tricks to ease the way. Here are three major lessons for winning the emotional game:

First Lesson: Don't feel bad about feeling bad. If you're frightened, lonely, out of sorts, don't think that there's something wrong with you for feeling that way. Leaving your family, friends, old neighborhoods, and familiar routines is an unpleasant experience. There would be something wrong with you if you faced all those things with a smile.

Accept the fact that you'll have bad moments and lonesome times. Don't multiply your own problems by telling yourself that you shouldn't have those feelings.

Second Lesson: Build a new family. A lot of the emotional pain surrounding folks at boot camp involves the loss of their families. Families can't be replaced. But with time and a little effort, you will make a valuable substitute. That will happen. You can hasten the moment by deliberately drawing people into your life.

Take the opportunities given you to learn a little more about the people around you. Why don't you be the one who sits down at lunch one day with one of the unit's loners? Why can't you be the one who introduces himself to a stranger during a break in training? Try to be just a little more outgoing than you think you naturally are. The results will surprise you.

Third Lesson: The fact that you're starting a new way of life doesn't mean you have to abandon everyone in your old life. Economize in other areas if that's what it takes to call the people who matter to you. See if you can master a military skill that isn't seen much any more: it's called "writing a letter."

FIVE SAYINGS FOR THE TOUGH TIMES

- "This only lasts a few weeks."
- "There are limits to what these people can do to me."
- "This only last a few weeks."
- "A quarter-million people survive this every year."
- "This only lasts a few weeks."

RULES, RULES, RULES

The military is a place of rules. There are rules for everything—what to wear, how to wear it, where to live, when to move, even whom you can socialize with during your own time. Perhaps not every rule makes sense all the time. But in a surprising number of instances, the reasons behind the rules make perfect sense. The regulations for promotions are ways to ensure equal treatment, while the rules governing assignments give people a framework around which they can plan their lives. Dress codes keep out the chaos that would follow if everyone could set their own appearance standards.

Many of the rules are inevitable in any organization the size of the U.S. armed forces. Imagine the confusion and the unfairness that would result if there weren't any hard-and-fast rules for deciding when military folks got pay raises. How could anyone fairly decide when each of 1.4 million people should get extra money in their paychecks? Answer: There's no way to do that fairly and individually. Hence the rules that usually give everyone in the military the same increase in pay every year, while other rules give the same basic pay to everyone in the same rank who has the same number of years in uniform.

More important than individual rules is the idea that everything about the military connects ultimately with combat, and combat is a group effort. Rules put predictability into the range of decisions that people can make under pressure.

The major tool for enforcing the military's rules is voluntary cooperation, and tens of millions of times every day, that's enough. People accept the fact that serving in uniform will take away some freedom and the right to make certain decisions. They do what they're supposed to, because they know that's a part of the career they choose to follow. It goes with the territory.

When, for whatever reason, people don't follow the rules, the military can haul out a variety of tools to bring them back into line. Those measures can range from counseling and extra duties to bad evaluations that would end chances for promotion and the best assignments. The military even operates its own legal system, which can try people for crimes unrelated to their military duties. Military courts have the authority to sentence someone's execution for a peacetime offense, although that hasn't happened in recent years.

RULES ON PERSONAL CONDUCT

"Straight-laced" isn't a phrase that Hollywood uses a lot to describe military life. Too often, the entertainment industry shows the armed forces as the last refuge in America for people who can't get along with others. But the reality is quite different from what pops up on the tube or the big screen.

"Values" is a word that's heard a lot on military bases, especially during boot camp. On active duty these days, there's little patience with rowdy behavior. Even though the services may be squeezed to get enough recruits, the military still insists that the men and women who wear the uniforms of the armed forces hold themselves to a high standard in their personal lives.

In chapter 12, we looked at some rules that apply to boot camp. Here are some general rules affecting personal conduct throughout the military.

Drug/Alcohol Abuse

The military has an absolute, no-exceptions, zero tolerance for illegal drugs, or for the abuse of legal drugs, such as prescription medicine. Whether the drugs are used off base on personal time without impacting upon a service member's duties is irrelevant. The military will come down hard upon offenders.

An equally tough attitude applies to military people whose performance is impaired by alcohol, either because they're tipsy or because they're hung over. Most commanders prohibit alcohol consumption before the start of the duty day or during it. Any drinking after duty that creates problems, either driving offenses or complaints from the neighbors that get back to the unit, will be dealt with firmly.

——————— ☆ ———————

"Colonel Purdy put up sign. This exceedingly civilized. Make it
very easy for uncivilized to know what not do to."

—Sakini (Marlon Brando) in
The Teahouse of the August Moon (MGM, 1956)

———————————

Protection from penalties is given to people who turn themselves in for treatment before the alcohol problems or drug use come to the notice of their commanders. They receive their full salaries during treatment, which is free.

Fraternization

Military organizations need clear lines separating professional lives from personal lives. "Fraternization" in a military sense describes any personal relationship that affects a vital professional relationship. Commanders don't socialize with the people in their units. Trainers must maintain purely professional ties with trainees. The military even discourages any sort of personal relationship between people of unequal rank who have on-the-job dealings.

Note that sex hasn't entered this discussion. When military folks talk about fraternization, they're not thinking about sexual relationships. Military people can have enormous power over their subordinates, and the organization is deeply concerned to make sure no one abuses that power. When it comes to sex, the military doesn't recognize consensual relations between commanders and subordinates, or between people of unequal rank in the same unit. Those sorts of relationship are prohibited. Period.

Sexual Harassment

Women are part of the military—always have been, always will be. In recent years, the military has taken stronger steps to make sure that they feel welcome. Commanders will come down hard on anyone who crosses the line with a military woman. Usually, that line is expressed as "unwanted sexual advances."

Too often, young people focus on the questions of what's "wanted" and what's "unwanted." That's the wrong part of the rule to look at. Instead, they need to understand that the heart of sexual harassment involves "sexual advances." That's touching, rubbing, kissing, suggestive gestures, lewd propositions, even dirty jokes. Stay away from that sort of activity, and you don't have to worry about the definition of "wanted."

The military is unique in its willingness to define some consensual relations as harassment. Any sexual relationship, in fact any personal relationship between certain groups of people, is prohibited in the military. Those situations include commanders (or anyone with authority) and subordinates, plus trainers and trainees.

People who feel that they are being sexually harassed—and, yes, that can include men—need to notify immediately someone in authority. That can include immediate bosses, chaplains, the investigators known as "inspectors general" (or IGs), or other senior military personnel.

Harassment

People come into the military with every sort of background. Everyone is welcome. Folks who give others a bad time because of something in their backgrounds will find themselves the target of official displeasure. Religious beliefs, political beliefs, race, ethnic makeup, gender, and sexual orientation are the sorts of things that should never be the subject of arguments, taunts, or derogatory remarks.

How can you know, in advance, what's going to offend someone? The answer is: You don't. But it's nearly impossible to be accused of harassment if you stick to work-related subjects.

Fighting

Military commanders don't want folks in their units who get into fights, either physical struggles where punches are thrown or the sort of thing in which people use words to wound. Belligerent people aren't good team

———— ☆ ————

"The force is with you, young Luke Skywalker. But you are not a Jedi yet."

—Darth Vader (David Prowse, voice of James Earl Jones) in *Star Wars: The Empire Strikes Back* (Twentieth Century Fox, 1980)

members, and the armed forces is one big team. It doesn't matter to the military whether the fights are on base, off base, with members of the military, or with civilians.

Even if they are cleared of criminal charges, people who are charged with violence by the military or by civilian authorities will likely find themselves denied promotions, choice assignments, and the best training. They can even be discharged from the armed forces.

Marriage

Folks in uniform don't need their commander's permission to marry. But the military has an interest in the marriages of service members. Some of the items that make up a military paycheck are larger for married people, and the spouses of active-duty folks are entitled to government health-care and other pricey benefits.

So the military will insist upon getting copies of marriage certificates. It will expect to be notified when marriages end, by receiving copies of divorce certificates. Marriages begin and end all the time, and the military's personnel and pay systems are used to coping with those changes. Only a few instances tend to cause troubles:

- Nontraditional marriages or divorces
- Gay or lesbian domestic partnerships
- Foreign marriages or divorces.

In this sense "nontraditional" means anything that's not usually recognized in society. Common-law marriages can qualify people for the military's benefits for spouses, but there are a lot of legal subtleties to those rules. Talk to a lawyer familiar with both military law and family law before going down that path.

Marriages between men and women of the same gender aren't recognized by the armed forces. Both marriages and divorces that take place under the laws of another country are another tricky area. Foreign marriages have to pass the muster of the Immigration and Naturalization Service. Proceed slowly; make sure commanders are aware of what's going on—they can tap the expertise of military lawyers and immigration experts.

Important Fine Print: Boyfriends and girlfriends don't meet the military's definition of "spouse" or "dependent," even if they're living with a military person, or they're totally dependent financially upon that person, or they've had a child with the military member.

Debts

In most of the working world, someone's personal finances are his or her own business. Not so in the military. People in uniform not supporting a family may be fraudulently receiving extra money from the military that's supposed to go to their families. Or it could mean they have become security risks. Or they may simply fall short of the military's standards for personal behavior.

Commanders can put a lot of pressure upon military folks who don't honor their debts. The military is especially tough upon people in uniform who don't live up to obligations for child support and alimony. When a court orders the military to dock someone's pay for debts, child support, or alimony, the military will do so. No one talks his or her way out of it.

Moonlighting

A military paycheck doesn't always take care of the bills. Also, many people in uniform find themselves with time on their hands after work that they'd just as soon fill with a second job that brings in extra income. Military people must check out off-duty jobs with their on-duty bosses.

Commanders have an interest in how members of their units spend their private time. If an off-duty job takes up too much time, puts an active-duty member in danger, or even reflects poorly upon the armed services, commanders have considerable authority to stop it. Units have their own rules that spell out the kinds of off-duty jobs that people can take, plus requirements for notifying superiors.

PROFESSIONAL RULES

The key issues affecting the working lives of people in uniform—promotions, assignments, living arrangements—are covered by layers of rules and regulations.

Often, Congress establishes the foundation for the military's handling of a particular policy by writing general provisions into federal law. The Defense Department takes that legislation and fills in many details about exactly how it will be met. The individual services, in turn, take the Pentagon's instructions and craft their own regulations, which get even more specific. Often, lesser headquarters will write their own rules, based upon all the guidance produced at the higher levels, narrowing the focus even more.

The intention of all this rule-writing is to give military people written instructions that tell them exactly how the policies affecting their professional lives will be carried out. Here, at a very broad level, are some of those policies.

Promotion

Everyone in uniform should have the chance to rise in rank to the best of their abilities. Such things as race and gender aren't supposed to be factors in promotions, and the military gets very tough even on senior officers when it looks as if those things played a part in deciding who gets higher rank. Most outside observers agree that the military has done a far better job treating its people equally in advancement than has much of the private sector.

Playing a part in promotions are evaluations, training, formal schooling, and assignments. Career fields can also be a limiting factor. Some military jobs that are expanding or experiencing turnover present better opportunities for promotion than fields for which everyone wants to volunteer.

As part of their promotion policy, the armed forces often use a rule that's known as "up or out." The idea is that people must continue advancing on the promotion ladder (going "up") or they'll be discharged (going "out"). That's why you don't see fifty-year-old people in the lowest ranks.

Assignments

Where people work has a lot to do with their satisfaction with their jobs. The folks running the armed forces understand this. They also know that the chance to travel brings many people into uniform. Then, as people get older and have children, they tend to lose their interest in travel and put a higher priority upon stability.

That gives the people overseeing military assignments an incredible balancing act. To the extent possible, the military tries to put people where they want to go, so long as it's a place needing someone of their rank and career field.

Four years tends to be the maximum that military folks stay in one place, although there are exceptions. Overseas assignments where family members cannot go are much shorter, usually around eighteen months. Navy, Coast Guard, and to some extent the Marine Corps try to equalize the amount of time everyone spends in shipboard assignments. How to spread the burden of combat fairly is still an issue the military is grappling with. During the Vietnam War, the last long-running conflict, the typical tour of duty in the war zone was a year.

Housing

The Pentagon is one of the few employers left who decides where people live. As a rule, enlisted people who are single and are also in the four lowest ranks (E-1 to E-4) must live on base if space is available. Single people in the four top enlisted ranks (E-6 to E-9) generally have the right to choose whether to live on or off base. Single E-5s are in a gray area where local rules prevail.

The rule for officers—single and married—is that they generally get to choose a home on base or in the civilian community, although there are exceptions. Married people, both officers and enlisted, usually get to live with their families, although there are exceptions involving sea duty and assignments for which the military says families shouldn't follow the person in uniform.

Medals

A big motivator for many folks in uniform are medals. They tell the world that someone has done an important job or has served in a tough spot. Medals can be a factor in promotions and assignments, although even then they're just one factor among many.

Essentially, medals are given for three reasons:

- Heroism
- Doing a good job
- Serving in a particular location.

The U.S. military is more generous with its medals than many of the world's other military forces. A typical enlisted person serving a few years on active duty can count on receiving a couple of medals.

The top medals for combat heroism can increase pay for active-duty folks by 10 percent, while the Medal of Honor carries a monthly allowance for life. The Purple Heart, which is given for combat wounds, establishes the right to be buried in certain military cemeteries. Decorations for folks who served in a combat zone can give them an edge when looking for a job in the federal civil service.

Retirement

Everyone who serves twenty years on active duty is entitled to a monthly retirement check from the military for the rest of their lives, along with medical care and certain benefits for their families. People who spent

———— ✭ ————

"I have your rental agreement right here. If you blow anything up,
it's coming out of your deposit."

—Sgt. Bilko (Steve Martin) in *Sgt. Bilko*
(Universal Studios, 1996)

some or all of their military careers in the reserves or National Guard also qualify for retired pay after twenty years, although a "year" for them isn't measured on the typical calendar. (See chapter 15 for more details about military retirements.)

Some people with less than twenty years can qualify for military retired pay if they were discharged under certain programs or left with certain disabilities. For them, it's made very clear when they're taking off their uniforms that they have the right to receive retirement checks.

Usually, people with at least eighteen years in uniform are allowed to stay a few more to earn retirement rights. Except for those with disability retirements, rank is used in computing retired pay. For a certain rank to count as the retired rank, people must hold it for periods of six months to three years, depending on the rank in question.

THE MILITARY LEGAL SYSTEM

Any idea that the U.S. Department of Defense is just another employer goes out the window when people confront the military's legal powers. The military operates its own legal system. It can impose fines, imprison, and even order executions.

It makes crimes of things that aren't criminal offenses in the civilian world, like "dereliction of duty" and "conduct unbecoming an officer." It even has its own system of lawyers (called "judge advocates general," or JAGs) and a network of rights and procedures. One of the nation's top criminal lawyers has said that the military's legal system gives more protection to the accused than any court system in the world.

Here are some of the major features of military law:

Uniform Code of Military Justice (UCMJ)

The basic law governing the military is actually part of federal law, written by Congress and changed only when Congress formally passes an amendment. That set of basic military laws is called the Uniform Code of Military Justice, or UCMJ. It spells out crimes, legal rights, and courtroom procedures.

The UCMJ covers everyone on active duty. It applies while they're on the job working for the government, and it covers them when they're off work and in a civilian community. Technically, military retirees are also subject to the UCMJ, although it hasn't been applied in recent decades.

Nonjudicial Punishment

Short of a formal trial, the military has a unique system for handling minor offenses. It goes by the jaw-breaking title of "nonjudicial punishment." More commonly, it's known as "Article 15" in the Army and Air Force, while the other services refer to it as a "Captain's Mast."

Essentially, it's a way for people to agree to accept a punishment without admitting that they are guilty. The punishments are limited to thirty days confinement to quarters, losing half of their pay for two months, or certain restrictions for sixty days.

Nonjudicial punishment doesn't involve courts and judges. It's something that happens between military folks and their commanders. Usually, the accused can decide not to accept the punishment and ask for a formal court-martial. People on sea duty don't always have the right to insist upon a court-martial.

Court-Martial

When someone is tried for an offense in the military—with prosecutors, defense lawyers, juries, witnesses, and all the legal trappings—it's called a court-martial. Most of the common rights of criminal defendants in the United States apply to military people going through a court-martial.

A court-martial can be used for purely military crimes, like missing a unit's movement or being absent without leave. It can also try people for more common crimes, like burglary, assault, even murder.

---------- ☆ ----------

"This is no longer a vacation. It's a quest."

—Clark Griswald (Chevy Chase) in
National Lampoon's Vacation (Warner Brothers, 1983)

Accused are entitled to free representation from military lawyers, they can pay for their own civilian lawyer, or they can try to have the government pay for a civilian lawyer. Most people choose the military's lawyers. They are familiar with court-martial procedures, and they are outside the military's usual command structure.

Still, the court-martial system is an integral part of the military. Commanders must authorize trials, and they must review and approve sentences. Commanders have certain rights to lessen sentences, although they cannot increase them.

Courts-martial come in several varieties—special, summary and general—names that relate to the rank of the commander and the kinds of sentences that can be imposed.

Trivia: When talking about more than one court-martial, put the "s" after "court," not "martial." The plural version is "courts-martial."

★ ★ 14 ★ ★

PAYCHECKS AND BENEFITS

Military people have a surprisingly complicated system for pay. They're eligible for dozens of different kinds of payments each month—money for enlisting, for reenlisting, for housing expenses, for travel expenses, for becoming a recruiter, for being in a combat zone, for taking a job where they wear civilian clothes, for becoming a doctor, for serving on a submarine, for serving on an airplane, for jumping from an airplane, for being in an undesirable assignment, for being separated from their families, for being with their families and, ultimately, for dying on active duty.

Each payment has a specific purpose. Usually, they're given to get jobs done that the military knows would go unfilled without an extra financial incentive. Some payments, like the housing and food allowances, date back to the days when the military was woefully underpaid and extra money was given to people who lived off base. Others payments, like the reimbursements for expenses of reassignment, are given because they're fair.

In computer lingo, the "default mode" for military payments is that they show up in your paycheck if you're entitled to them. Usually, there's nothing you have to do to get them. But it's good to know what's out there.

PAY BASICS

Military pay is governed by federal laws that are written by Congress and implemented by the Defense Department. "One size fits all" is the general rule. Two people with the same rank, same number of years on active duty, assigned to the same base, with the same duties should receive the same amount of money, even if they're in different services.

Payday comes at the end of a month, and if military folks notify their pay office, at midmonth too. The size of the midmonth payment is up to the military member. Usually, the payment is made electronically to a soldier's bank account.

Most—but not all—of the items making up a military paycheck are taxable. Most of the time—but not always—military people have to pay taxes on their military income. For more, see the section below, "Taxes."

Basic Pay

Almost everyone on active duty receives Basic Pay. It's the closest the military gets to a salary. The handful of people who don't receive Basic Pay lost it as part of a court-martial conviction.

The amount of Basic Pay is determined by a person's rank and the number of years on active duty. Under the year 2000 pay scale, a recruit earned $930 per month. At the other end of the scale, a four-star general or admiral earned $10,655 monthly.

Usually, Congress increases Basic Pay for everyone each year when it approves a new Pentagon budget.

Housing Allowances

If the military doesn't provide a room for you to sleep in, it will pay you to rent or buy a place to stay in a civilian community.

Officers, and enlisted people E-6 and higher, usually have the option of choosing whether to live on base in government housing (which means they don't receive any housing allowance) or to live off base in a civilian community (in which case, they are paid the extra money).

The housing allowances have separate rates for people in each rank at each location. Within each rank, there are different rates for people with families and for those without.

———— ★ ————

"All I ever wanted was an honest week's pay for an honest day's work."

—Sgt. Bilko (Steve Martin) in *Sgt. Bilko*
(Universal Studios, 1996)

——————— ✫ ———————

"Something wrong with your meal?"

"Yes, sergeant. It's the first food I was afraid of."

—Sgt. Toomey (Christopher Walken) and Don Carney
(Casey Siemaszko) in *Biloxi Blues*
(Universal Studios, 1988)

The housing allowance that goes to people living in the states is the Basic Allowance for Housing (BAH). Overseas it is called the Overseas Housing Allowance (OHA).

Both the stateside and the overseas allowances are monthly additions to a military paycheck. The overseas allowance is a maximum payment: people only receive as much in OHA payments as they spend on housing costs, up to the maximum. The stateside allowance isn't affected by actual expenses. If your housing expenses are less than your housing allowance, you can pocket the difference.

Warning: The housing allowances underwent a major overhaul in 1998. Before that time, everyone on active duty—officer and enlisted—received a fixed housing allowance, while most people living off base received a second, add-on allowance that varied widely in size. Be careful taking advice from people who left the military before that change took place.

Food Allowances

As with housing, the rule with food is that if the military doesn't feed you, it will give you extra money to purchase your own food. This food money is called the Basic Allowance for Subsistence (BAS).

Officers have a simple BAS system. Officers receive a flat monthly amount, from which they must pay for any meals they receive from the government in a mess hall, aboard ship, or in the field. In the year 2000, the officers' BAS was $157 monthly.

Enlisted people can receive three different amounts of BAS, depending upon their circumstances. Enlisted BAS is calculated on a daily basis.

The most common enlisted BAS goes to people on leave and those who've been given permission not to eat in the mess hall, usually E-7s and higher-ranking personnel. For them, the 2000 rate was $7.50 a day. (This BAS rate is also known as "separate rations," which is shortened to "seprats.")

When no government dining facility is located where an enlisted person works, the BAS rate in 1999 was $8.46 daily. In certain high-cost areas, the rate can be $11.21 daily.

THE TAXMAN STILL COMETH

It may seem silly for the government to pay you one minute, then take back some of that money in taxes the next minute. But, as a rule, that's exactly what happens to military people. You may feel like a warrior, but to the IRS, you're just another taxpayer.

Federal income taxes, Social Security taxes, and Medicare taxes all usually come out of military paychecks. There are exceptions. One involves certain kinds of military pay that are always tax-free. The other involves folks in a combat zone. We'll discuss both exceptions shortly.

State income taxes can also be taken from active-duty paychecks, but that can be tricky. If your military pay falls into one of the two tax-free exceptions to federal income tax, then you don't have to pay state income taxes. If you live on a military installation, you pay state taxes to your home state, not the state in which you live. The rules can be different for people living off base. When in doubt, check with your base's legal office.

As noted a few paragraphs ago, some kinds of military pay are always free from taxes. The good news is that you don't have to worry about the details; the military does that for you. If a certain kind of pay is tax exempt, then the military doesn't include it with the taxable pay listed on your W-4, the form used to compute your federal taxes.

For the record, the following categories of military pay are always free from taxes, including federal, state, Social Security and Medicare:

- Housing allowances
- Subsistence allowances
- Clothing allowances
- Per diem payments
- Reassignment reimbursements
- Uniform allowances.

As we mentioned earlier, all military pay can be shielded from income taxes when people in uniform are stationed in certain international hotspots. This is called "the combat-zone exclusion." One piece of fine print is crucial: the combat-zone exclusion begins when the president signs a paper called an executive order that says, in effect, "Military people serving in the following areas don't have to pay taxes."

The combat-zone exclusion isn't connected in any way with getting hazardous duty pay or even combat pay. Getting shot at doesn't qualify you for tax-free military money.

As this book went to press, only two places qualified for tax protection under the combat-zone exclusion—the portion of the Middle East around Iraq where U.S. troops have been stationed since the Persian Gulf War, and the former Yugoslavia, where U.S. forces have served in a variety of peacekeeping missions since the mid-1990s.

When enlisted people qualify for this combat-zone tax protection, all of their military pay earned in the combat zone is exempted from federal and state income tax. Officers have only a portion of their pay protected from taxes; everything above that limit is taxed. The limit is equal to the highest enlisted pay, which, as this book went to press, was about $4,500 per month. This means that the first $4,500 in monthly pay for officers covered by the combat-zone exclusion is shielded from taxes, while everything above that limit is taxed.

HERE SOME PAY, THERE SOME PAY

By one count, the military has more than fifty different kinds of pay. The book that gives just the basics about pay, *The Military Pay Manual*, is several hundred pages long. Each of the services maintains thousands of pages of regulations that give more details.

Fortunately for people in uniform, the only ones who have to master that information work for the government as payroll experts. None of the dozens of kinds of military pay require you to apply for them. If you're eligible for extra money, the personnel folks know it, and they'll see that it's added to your paycheck.

For the record, let's review some of the most common additions to a military paycheck, giving amounts and eligibility rules. Readers should be warned that many of these amounts change and that the eligibility rules are only a summary. Unless expressed differently, all amounts are monthly rates:

Diving Pay: $150–$300. For trained, full-time, military-assigned divers. Enlisted only.

Family Separation Allowance: $150. When government won't pay to move families to new assignments, usually overseas.

Flight Pay: $125–$840. Enlisted crewmembers get minimum. Highest amounts to pilots, navigators, others in cockpit.

Foreign Duty Pay: $8–$20. For overseas assignment. Rates based on rank.

Hazardous Duty Pay: $150. For assignment to specific, qualifying skills.

High-cost of Living Allowance: averages about $60. Extra money for living in highest-cost areas within the states. Called "Conus COLA."

Hostile Fire Pay: $150. For assignment to combat zone or duties in which combat is likely.

Imminent Danger Pay: $150. For assignments where combat is likely.

Nuclear Pay: Up to $15,000 a year. Only for officers trained to run nuclear power plants.

Parachute Pay: $150. For people assigned to full-time parachute duty who take minimum monthly jumps.

Per Diem: Varies widely. Daily add-ons for housing and food for temporary duty in high-cost areas.

Reenlistment Bonuses: Up to $45,000 total. Incentive to stay on active duty. Rates determined by skill, service, manpower needs.

Sea Pay: $50–$520. For shipboard duty. Rates vary by rank and years of sea duty. Must be at least E-4.

Submarine Pay: $75–$595. For people assigned to submarines or in training. Rates based on rank and time in service.

Uniform Allowance: $187–$425 yearly. To purchase and repair uniforms. Rates vary by service, time in uniform, gender. Enlisted only. Junior enlisted get uniforms, not money.

WHEN THE DOCTOR CALLS

The U.S. military exists to fight. By being strong enough to prevail on any battlefield, the military has been able to deter other nations from attacking us.

Nowhere is the hard-nosed reality behind the armed forces clearer—in its generosity and its toughness—than when it comes to medical care.

Everyone on active duty receives free medical care. Period. There are no charges for doctor visits, hospital stays, X-rays, prescription medicine, dental work, or glasses. If a hospital operated by another service in your area has a specialist you need, you'll be sent there. If only a major military hospital like Walter Reed Army Medical Center in Washington, D.C., or Bethesda Naval Medical Center has the specialists necessary to put you back on your feet, you'll be referred there.

Only in absolute medical emergencies are active-duty people treated by nonmilitary health professionals. Even then, the government pays the bill.

Unlike almost all civilian employers, the military doesn't limit active-duty people to a set number of "sick" days per year. If you're in the military and you're ill, you get the problem fixed. There's no limit on the number of days you can miss work. However many days you miss, it doesn't affect your regular vacation days, called "annual leave" in the military.

That's the good news for the people in uniform. There's also some less-than-good news: the military is for healthy people. If you have a medical problem that can't be cured and that will affect your readiness for combat, you'll be discharged.

People discharged with medical problems usually qualify for free, life-time care from the Department of Veterans Affairs (the VA) and also for monthly disability pay. More about people leaving active duty with medical problems is in chapter 19.

That single-minded focus upon keeping our fighting forces in tip-top shape means that everyone else—spouses, children, retirees, and their families—receive treatment after the people in uniform are attended to.

As a practical matter, no sick child is going to be left untreated in a military emergency room because some active-duty person needs a flu shot. That military-comes-first mentality usually means that family members may be encouraged to go to off-base health professionals. As discussed in chapter 16, a number of government programs help offset the costs of their private care.

THEN, WHEN DUTY CALLS

Reassignment orders are a fact of military life. Every couple of years, active-duty people are told to report to another installation, unit, or vessel. They may even be sent to another country.

Uprooting your life is tough. Military people don't like being separated from their families, old neighborhoods, and daily routines. Most come to see those reassignments as trade-offs. For the aggravation of moving to a strange place, their military career gets a boost, and they get to spend time in a part of the country—or a portion of the world—they wouldn't otherwise see.

For its part, the military tries to make those transfers as easy as possible. The government will pay to get you and your worldly goods to your new assignment. People going to boot camp and to the bases where they learn their basic military skills may be handed an airline ticket and the name of a moving company that will ship their personal possessions at government expense.

Once enlistees and new officers get beyond their initial training, a more generous range of benefits kicks in whenever they receive transfer orders. It includes:

Dislocation Allowance: Varies by rank. In the year 2000, it ranged from about $520 to $2,610.

Mileage Allowance: At least fifteen cents per mile to drive the family car to the new assignment.

Per Diem: $50 per day for each adult traveling to the new assignment.

Temporary Lodging Allowance: Extra money if on-base housing isn't immediately available after arriving at the new base.

For most people, the costly part of moving involves shipping their personal stuff. The military refers to the stuff as "household goods," whether it involves a couple of footlockers or several rooms' worth of furniture.

The government will pay to ship household goods from the old assignment to the new. But there are limits. The limits are based on the weight of the material. Different ranks have their own weight limits, and within each rank there are often separate rates for people with families and those without families.

Usually, when two people on active duty who are married to each other are reassigned at the same time to the same new location, they can add together their individual weight allowances to come up with a single weight limit for their family. But when both active-duty partners are E-1s, E-2s, or E-3s and they have no other dependents, the couple is limited to a single five-thousand-pound shipment.

Household Goods Weight Allowance (in pounds)

Rank	With Dependents	Without Dependents
O-6 & higher	18,000	18,000
O-5 & W-5	17,500	16,000
O-4 & W-4	17,000	14,000
O-3 & W-3	14,500	13,000
O-2 & W-2	13,500	12,500
O-1 & W-1	12,000	10,000
E-9	14,500	12,000
E-8	13,500	11,000
E-7	12,500	10,500
E-6	11,000	8,000
E-5	9,000	7,000
E-4 (more than 2 yrs)	8,000	7,000
E-4 (2 yrs or less)	7,000	3,500
E-3	5,000	2,000
E-2	5,000	1,500
E-1	5,000	1,500

———— ☆ ————

"You don't go on sick call with these guys unless a tank runs over you."

—Joseph Wykowski (Matt Mulhern) in *Biloxi Blues*
(Universal Studios, 1988)

———————————

Sometimes, government business takes military people away from the places they are normally assigned. This is called "temporary duty" or "temporary additional duty." Military people on temporary duty receive extra money to cover the costs of buying meals in restaurants and sleeping in hotels.

The rates for temporary duty payments are set for each community, based upon local costs. It can consist of a meals allowances, which varies from thirty to forty-two dollars daily, plus a lodging allowance. Usually, the lodging allowance is a maximum payment, which means you get less if your costs are less. The meals allowance is a flat-rate item, meaning you receive a certain amount of money, regardless of your actual costs.

OTHER PERKS OF MILITARY LIFE

Many military installations are self-contained cities, with a wide range of recreational, cultural, and educational facilities. You never have to leave the base unless you want a change of pace.

Here are a few programs of special interest:

On-Base Stores

All but the smallest installations have "exchanges," which are the military's version of a department store, and "commissaries," which are food stores.

Across the board, exchanges and commissaries offer better prices than off-base stores can offer. Neither one has a sales tax, and neither operates at a profit.

But that's not to say that everything in every exchange and commissary costs less than everything in the off-base Wal-Mart or Safeway. Civilian merchants offer some items at a loss to draw customers into their stores. That gives even more opportunities for savings for the savvy military shopper.

Education

One of the major reasons that people join the military is to further their educations. Pentagon leaders understand this. They also believe that the military has an obligation to advance the education of its people, even if that schooling has nothing to do with military skills.

Each of the services has a variety of programs that bring civilian teachers on base for after-hours classes. Military supervisors are also tolerant when it comes to excusing troops from their duties to attend civilian classes. Military duties always come first, however, and commanders won't approve any classes that get in the way of a unit's training or combat readiness.

The deal that many nonveterans don't understand is called "tuition assistance." It's money from the military to pay the bills to attend civilian classes. The armed forces will pay all of the costs of getting a high school diploma and up to 75 percent of the costs of getting bachelor's and master's degrees.

The tuition assistance program doesn't commit people to spend more time in uniform, and it doesn't subtract from their benefits under the GI Bill educational program. Tuition assistance isn't a guaranteed right, however, and it's not unusual for the program to run out of money, forcing service members to delay signing up for classes or to pay from their own pockets.

For more than fifty years, the military's most popularly known educational program has been the GI Bill. It has gone by many names, and many different rule books, since its inception during the height of World War II. The latest version is called the Montgomery GI Bill, after its author, former Congressman Sonny Montgomery. Unlike earlier versions of the GI Bill, the Montgomery GI Bill requires a contribution from military people. You have to contribute a hundred dollars a month for your first twelve months on active duty. In return, you'll receive about $450 a month for educational expenses for thirty-six months, for a total of more than $19,000.

The Montgomery GI Bill doesn't have many rules, but the ones that it has are pretty inflexible:

- You must contribute the hundred dollars a month for all twelve months. You can't offer more for a greater pay-out, or less for less money.
- The payment—called a "withholding"—must be made during your first twelve months on active duty. If you turn the offer down when it's offered at boot camp, you can't change your mind later.
- You pick the school you want to attend with GI Bill money. But the government may refuse to pay if the school is a "diploma mill," a nonaccredited institution.
- If you don't use your GI Bill benefits, you can't get back your $1,200 contribution.

A rule that has some flexibility is a ten-year deadline. Generally, payments under the Montgomery GI Bill program end ten years after a veteran leaves the military. Exceptions are common when illness or hardship prevents the former service member from going to school for a while after discharge.

People on active duty can use their Montgomery GI Bill benefits; it's not only for veterans who have left the services. In fact, it's common for folks attending classes with money from tuition assistance to dip into their GI Bill education benefits to help out when the tuition assistance money runs dry.

Housing

Also associated with former military folks are GI Bill home loans. That program, like GI Bill educational assistance, is also open to people who are still in uniform.

GI Bill home loans used to have a substantially better interest rate than other mortgages. That isn't true any more. The main advantage of the program is that mortgage lenders don't usually require down payments. Still, a typical home purchase under the GI Bill can involve more than a thousand dollars in various fees.

The government can't negotiate the price of a home, nor does the government guarantee its quality. But one benefit for veterans is that VA inspectors examine the house. They won't give it the government's seal of approval if it's unfairly priced or in poor repair.

To qualify, people now in uniform must serve at least 180 days continuously on active duty. Once you've passed the 180-day mark, you can apply for a GI Bill home loan. Reservists who don't meet the 180-day rule must wait until they've spent six years in the reserves or National Guard before taking advantage of this program.

We refer to this program as "GI Bill home loans," although the phrase isn't accurate. The government doesn't give mortgages to veterans: the government makes a promise to the banks and financial institutions that give people the mortgages. The promise is that the government will protect the financial institutions from some of their losses if the veterans or military people fail to keep up with payments.

This is one government program in which the private sector has a considerable voice. Since veterans buy homes with money lent by banks and various financial institutions, those lenders have a say in deciding whether a particular veteran can repay the home loan. When they decide a veteran doesn't make enough to pay back the loan, the government rarely intervenes.

Using the GI Bill to buy a house is easier than using it to take classes. Step One: Find a house you like. Step Two: Tell the real estate agent, bank, or mortgage company that you're a veteran. Step Three: Fill out the forms that they're happy to provide.

★ ★ 15 ★ ★

RETIREMENT

For most people, the military is a place to spend a few years. They come on active duty, go through training, take transfer orders that send them to a couple of different places, and then return to the civilian world.

For a small percentage, however, the military becomes a career. They devote their working lives to the armed forces. Eventually, however, they reach a point where they—or the military—decide that they've done enough. They take off their uniforms for the last time. They become military retirees.

For having served their country for so long, these people receive military retired pay for their rest of their lives. Most find that military retired pay is better than anything available in the private sector for the same education, skills, and time on the job. Military retirees are also eligible for a range of on-base benefits and programs.

Society often accords them a special status. Most retirees are known for the rest of their lives as "master sergeant" or "major," not "mister" or "missus."

WHO CAN RETIRE?

There's a magic number that comes into play for military retirement. The number is twenty. Most people must stay on active duty for twenty years to become military retirees.

Everyone who passes that mark will get military retired pay. It's guaranteed by federal law. Retirees receive a monthly check from the government, plus health-care benefits, lifetime access to on-base commissaries and exchanges.

There are some exceptions to this rule.

Early Retirements

Some good performers in uniform have skills that aren't in high demand by the military anymore. They have the desire to stay for twenty years; they may be more than three-quarters of the way there; but the military simply doesn't need them.

In some cases, the government can offer an early retirement to people with at least fifteen years on active duty. There's a key detail here: service members don't have a *right* to retire after fifteen years, but they can retire if they're selected by commanders who are trying to reduce the number of people on active duty.

The early retirement program goes by several names. "Fifteen-year retirement" is one, although that can be misleading, since people retire under this program with sixteen, seventeen, eighteen and even nineteen years in uniform. Another name is "TERA retirements." The acronym stands for "Temporary Early Retirement Authority," which can be misleading, too. People who receive early retirements are permanently retired. It can't be taken away. What's "temporary" is the military's legal authority to start people on these early retirements.

Disability Retirements

Being physically fit is essential to being in the military. When illness or injury limit a person's ability to serve in uniform, the government will print a set of discharge orders and send that person back to the civilian world.

The military is hard-nosed about fitness for duty—but not heartless. Every year, thousands of people receive disability retirements from the armed forces. They are retirees just like the twenty-year people, and they're eligible for the same range of benefits.

As a rule, the people receiving military disability retirements tend to have at least eight years on active duty. Generally, people with less time in uniform receive a one-time, lump-sum payment called "disability severance pay."

Everyone with medical problems related to military service is eligible to apply for VA disability compensation (discussed in chapter 18).

Yes, the programs overlap. Yes, it's possible to receive military disability retired pay and VA disability compensation at the same time. But for every

———— ✫ ————

"It took me 30 or 40 years to get the hang of it. Now that everything's going smooth, [retirement] would be throwing away my training."

—Marty Maher (Tyrone Power) in *The Long Gray Line*
(Columbia, 1955)

———————————

dollar of VA money, the government will withhold one dollar of military money.

Only those who leave the military with "retired" stamped on their discharge papers are considered military retirees.

Reserve Retirements

Active duty isn't the only route to a military retirement. Men and women must shoulder the part-time responsibilities of members of the reserves and National Guard. As an incentive, the military offers them a retirement, too.

Determining who's eligible for reserve retirements is more difficult than finding that out for an active-duty member. The formulas for calculating the amount of reserve retired pay are also more difficult.

Most reservists and guardsmen spend one weekend each month on their military duties, plus two full weeks each year. It takes twenty years of that routine to qualify for retired pay as a reservist or National Guardsman.

The amount of retired pay earned by twenty years of part-time reserve service isn't as large as the amount paid for twenty years of full-time, active-duty time. Reservists and National Guardsmen begin receiving their retired pay on their sixtieth birthdays.

The Flip Side: We've been talking about people who can retire. There's another group with a different problem. They are the people who *must* retire.

Except for the most senior generals, admirals, E-9s, and people with the rarest technical skills, most people must retire by the time they have thirty years on active duty. Few people even make it to the thirty-year mark. The services have rules that dictate when certain people must retire. Those rules are based upon rank.

Generally, majors and lieutenant commanders must retire at twenty years; the same with E-6s. Colonels, navy captains, and E-8s must retire at thirty years. Mandatory retirement dates for the other ranks are spaced between the twenty-year and thirty-year marks.

Reality Check: "Retired," in this instance, doesn't mean "sitting at home and doing nothing." Collecting a military retired paycheck doesn't prevent anyone from holding a regular, postmilitary job. Folks don't lose any retired pay because they collect a paycheck from a private-sector employer or even if they take a job with the federal civil service.

A typical enlisted retiree is thirty-eight when the retirement checks begin. That's young enough to start a second career. In fact, most military retirees find that their retired pay alone isn't enough to pay their bills, especially when they're younger and have families. They have to keep working.

RETIRED PAY

Military retirees receive monthly checks from the government based upon their rank and the number of years they spent in uniform.

As discussed earlier, slightly different rules are in effect for active-duty retirees and people retiring from the reserves and National Guard. There are also subtle differences between people whose military careers started after September 8, 1980, and those who put on a uniform for the first time before that date.

Here are some general principles about military retired pay:

- It provides a monthly check for the lifetime of the retiree.
- It ends upon the death of the retiree.
- It increases to keep pace with inflation, usually every year.
- It's taxable (an exception is made for people disabled in combat).
- It isn't reduced when retirees get a civilian job or earn an income. (There are exceptions for people drawing VA disability pay.)

The formulas for calculating retired pay are designed to give more money to people who stay longer in uniform. But the formulas stop at thirty years. That means that an E-9 who retires this year after thirty years in uniform will receive the same amount of monthly retired pay as an E-9 who retires this year after 35 years on active duty.

A major or lieutenant commander who retired in 1999 with twenty years on active duty received $2,283 in monthly retired pay. For an E-6 (staff sergeant, petty officer first class, or technical sergeant) retiring in 1999 with twenty years active duty time, the monthly retired pay was $1,086. Again, those monthly payments usually increase every year at the same rate as inflation.

How is it calculated? Keep in mind that we're talking here about the system for active-duty retirements, not reservists, National Guardsmen, or disabled folks.

For someone whose military career starts this year, the government will add the Basic Pay—not total pay—for the retiree's top thirty-six months on active duty. That figure is then divided by thirty-six to produce a monthly average. A twenty-year retiree gets 50 percent of that average Basic Pay. The percentage increases by 2.5 percent for each additional year on active duty, for a maximum of 75 percent of the average Basic Pay after thirty years.

For active-duty folks, retired pay starts immediately upon retiring from the military.

Reserve Retirements

A slightly different system is in effect for people who retire from the reserves and National Guard.

Besides rank and years in the military, a third thing is used to compute their retired pay: "points." A reservist gets one point for being on active duty for one day and two points for attending a day's drill at the armory. Other points are awarded for things like correspondence courses.

Some fine print is very important here. Twenty years in the reserves isn't enough to qualify for retirement; it must be twenty years in which the service member earned at least fifty points. If they don't earn fifty points during a twelve-month period, the time doesn't count toward their retirement.

Here's how a reserve retirement is calculated for people whose military career starts now. Their total points will be added together, then divided by 360. That figure is multiplied by 0.025. The result is multiplied by the average Basic Pay in effect for thirty-six months before retirement.

It doesn't yield nearly as much as an active-duty retirement. Let's take the example of an E-6 who retired in 1999 and has twenty years in the reserves, each year earning the minimum of fifty points. That person's

———— ☆ ————

"You come out here city slickers. You're going to go home cowboys."

—Clay Stone (Noble Willingham) in *City Slickers*
(MGM, 1991)

monthly retired pay would be about $150. Again, that assumes the minimum points. A typical reserve E-6 would have at least two or three times that number of points.

One further thing about the retired pay for reservists and National Guardsmen is quite different than that of retirees from active duty: they receive their first check for retired pay on their sixtieth birthdays. It doesn't begin immediately after leaving the military.

Reality Check: "Erosion of benefits" and "whittling away" are phrases used by many old soldiers talking about retired pay. Those statements can be misleading.

Military retired pay has never been taken away from anyone to save the government money. Nor have individual retirees seen the size of their retired pay shrink from one year to the next. The cutbacks that some retirees complain about have involved, principally, changes in government-paid health care.

Yes, those changes have meant that some retirees had less money to spend on other things. But their retired pay didn't decrease.

Sometimes, as part of government-wide austerity programs, Congress has approved cost-of-living increases in military retired pay that don't keep up with inflation. That erodes spending power. But it's not the same thing as Congress approving cutbacks in the amounts of retired pay, which some folks seem to imply happens.

RETIRED RULES

Being in the military is like being in no other job in the country. In the same way, being a retired soldier is like being no other kind of retiree.

Military retirees are governed by some special rules long after they take off their uniforms. Frankly, most of those rules limit what they can do. They're not awful; they're just not positive. Let's start with the one that has the most upbeat features.

Veterans Preference

The federal government gives a special advantage at hiring time to men and women who have served in the military. So do most state and municipal governments, along with many corporations. It's called a "veterans preference."

It's not a guaranteed job, just an edge when decisions are made to add people to the payroll. The preference usually takes the form of a few extra points in selection formulas that assign points for education, work experience, and skills.

Unfortunately, none of the formal veterans preference programs single out retirees. Put another way, any veterans preference a military retiree qualifies for also applies to former military folks who are nonretirees. In fact, the federal government's preferences don't apply to retired officers in the rank of major, lieutenant commander or higher, unless they also have disabilities.

Even then, many perfectly healthy majors and lieutenant commanders are members of the federal civil service. They got their jobs without needing the extra advantage of a veterans preference.

"Double Dipping"

For decades, there were limitations on the income of military retirees when they took second careers as federal civil servants. That situation was called "double dipping," or more formally, "dual compensation."

Congress abolished all restrictions in 1999. Now, military retirees can collect their full retired pay, plus their full civil service salaries. But the memory of those rules lingers. Be wary of advice you receive from old soldiers and old publications.

Second Careers

Most people are comparatively young when they begin receiving military retired pay. They need to continue working. As far as the government is concerned, they can work wherever they can find a job.

Only in a few instances does the government impose any restrictions upon where a military retiree can work. People who represented the government in dealings with private industry cannot go to work for those industries immediately after leaving active duty. Some face a time limit, others are barred for life.

---------------- ✯ ----------------

"You've done enough damage, Rambo. This mission is over."

—Col. Samuel Trautman (Richard Crenna) in
First Blood (Artisan Entertainment, 1982)

A tougher ban involves foreign governments. There's a provision in the U.S. Constitution that legal scholars say prohibits military retirees from working for any foreign government. (Article 1, Section 9: "No person holding any office of profit or trust . . . shall . . . accept any present . . . from any . . . foreign state.") In fact, U.S. military retirees can lose their retired pay if they give up their U.S. citizenship.

Recall

Technically, military retirees can be recalled to active duty, at any age, for a national emergency. As a practical matter, the only retirees who come back into uniform are those who want to. But, for the record, the law is on the books.

UCMJ

Military retirees are also, strictly speaking, subject to the provisions of the Uniform Code of Military Justice. They can be brought back on active duty and tried for their misdeeds, even if the charges have nothing to do with their military service. At least, that's what the federal law says.

As a practical matter, it doesn't happen. No country where military courts try civilians enjoys popular support, and U.S. officials don't want to start down that road. Crimes committed while on active duty, but detected after retirement, don't go unpunished. They go into the federal criminal-justice system.

★ ★ 16 ★ ★

SPOUSES, CHILDREN, EX-SPOUSES, SURVIVORS

Uncle Sam isn't your ordinary employer. He's one boss who can order you to pack up at a moment's notice and move halfway around the world into a combat zone. Working for Uncle Sam also has its pluses. A military job surpasses those in the private sector in the benefits available to an employee's (in this case, a military member's) family.

The spouses, children, and, under very stringent rules, other people in the family of someone on active duty can qualify for free medical care in hospitals and clinics on base, plus reduced-fee treatment off base. Family members receive money to cover the expense of government-ordered moves. They're eligible for a full range of on-base activities, from shopping in base exchanges and commissaries to using military lawyers and signing up for on-base swimming pools.

One catch about these family benefits is important for young people. The military has its own definition of "family," and it's pretty old fashioned. Girlfriends and boyfriends don't qualify. There's no wiggle room in the rules to squeeze them through, even if you're living with them and paying all the bills. A child you have with a boyfriend or girlfriend can qualify for military benefits, but in order to promote your significant other to the officially recognized status of "military family member," you'll need a marriage licence.

SPOUSES AND CHILDREN

The military has its own word for spouses and children who meet its definition of "family members." They're called "dependents."

In the vast majority of cases, there's no question about who's a dependent. The man or woman you married and live with is a dependent, as are the children you brought into the world and now support. They're given military ID cards that guarantee access to on-base facilities, including hospitals and clinics.

Parents can qualify as military dependents if they're living apart from the person on active duty. But it's not easy. There are many rules for them. The most important—and difficult one to satisfy—is that the soldier must pay for more than half of the dependent's living expenses.

Here are some of the major benefits involving family members:

Extra Pay

The Defense Department is one of the few employers anymore who increases employees' pay when they marry. The extra money comes in the housing-related allowances—the Basic Allowance for Housing (BAH), Overseas Housing Allowance (OHA), and overseas Cost-of-Living Allowance (COLA). There are no changes in the financial foundation of the military paycheck—Basic Pay—or in the food allowance (the Basic Allowance for Subsistence, or BAS) when military people marry.

Note: The extra money that a person in uniform gets because there's an official dependent in the household doesn't go directly to the spouse or child. It goes to the military person. It's up to the service member to ensure that the money is used on the dependent's behalf.

Health Care

The families of active-duty people can get health insurance from the government to cover most medical bills, in the same way that the families of civilian workers are covered by employer-sponsored health-insurance plans.

For military families, the plan is called "TriCare." It is better than the programs offered by many civilian employers. Military people don't pay pre-

---- ★ ----

"With intrepid pioneering spirit, the Robinson family will journey
to the distant world of Alpha Prime."

—Announcer in *Lost in Space*
(New Line Cinema, 1998)

miums every month for TriCare. They make minimal payments for medical service. For example, in 1999, the out-of-pocket costs were five dollars for prescription drugs and six dollars for each visit to a civilian doctor.

Under certain conditions, spouses and children can get free treatment in military hospitals and clinics on base. The key phrase is "space available." If military doctors have openings in their schedules and treatment rooms aren't being used by active-duty patients, then spouses and children can be treated in those on-base facilities. But first priority for on-base care always goes to the man or woman wearing the uniform. The military can be very hard-nosed on this point.

On-Base Services

A wide array of services and stores are available at most military installations for people who qualify as "dependents," including:

- The tax-free grocery stores (commissaries) and department stores (exchanges). You may be able to find some items cheaper off base. But, on average, you'll save money shopping in commissaries and exchanges.
- Recreational facilities (called "morale, welfare and recreation" facilities, or MWR). They include gymnasiums, movie theaters, woodworking shops, auto-repair shops, libraries, bowling alleys, tennis courts, swimming pools and other programs.
- Experts, including legal assistance, chaplains, employment counselors and others. Family-oriented help from chaplains and Red Cross officials is free and easily available for all family members of active-duty folks. Other assistance, such as that of legal experts and job counselors, may depend upon active-duty folks getting help first, with spouses and children being served if the experts have time.

Government Housing

The government can put additional money into the paychecks of active-duty people if they are unable to get on-base housing and if they have family members who qualify as dependents. Or the government can authorize on-base housing large enough to accommodate a soldier's dependents. On-base housing is considered to be free, although it usually has a hidden cost. Military folks normally lose a portion of a typical military paycheck—the Basic Allowance for Housing (BAH)—when they move into military-provided housing.

This is one issue covered with fine print. Some of it shows up in basic training camp. You may have an official dependent, but the government will still expect you to sleep in the barracks. Or the military might not authorize your dependents to move into government housing while you're at boot camp or, later in your career, at some remote overseas assignments.

Moving

When military people are reassigned, the government usually picks up the costs of moving their spouses, children, and others who meet the official dependent definition. But sometimes—boot camp is a common example—the military doesn't want the family members to be there, so the government won't pay their travel costs.

When Uncle Sam is willing to move family members, the extra money actually goes to the person on active duty, not directly to the family members. Payments include certain amounts for food and lodging for each dependent, plus travel costs. The government can provide military members and their families with tickets that will get them to the new assignment.

Downside: Commanders aren't shy about sticking their noses into the private lives of people in uniform. The military man (or woman) who isn't taking care of the family can get into serious trouble with the government. This is especially true when extra money is paid for the housing or travel expenses of a spouse or children, and those payments clearly aren't being used for their benefit. Careers end, and sometimes military people go to jail, because of this kind of family problem.

Reminder: We've been talking about government benefits for the families of people on active duty. Those benefits are layered with rules. The first rule is that the military decides who is recognized as an official family member, or dependent. Boyfriends and girlfriends never qualify.

EX-SPOUSES, ALIMONY, CHILD SUPPORT

Just as the military takes an official interest whenever someone in uniform acquires a husband, wife or a child, it also gets involved whenever someone loses one.

Keep in mind that some military payments are increased for folks with families. Other benefits, like the military ID card and access to military-subsidized health insurance, are limited to people who meet the official definition of a dependent.

So, the government wants to know when you don't have a family any more. To be safe, everyone facing divorce or separation should talk the situation over with their immediate military superiors and the folks in the

———————— ☆ ————————

"War changes people."

"War doesn't make you rude to your parents."

—Karen Collier (Kimberly Williams) and
Maurine Collier (Kathy Bates) in *The War at Home*
(Touchstone Pictures, 1996)

———————————————

personnel office. Make sure you—or someone else—aren't getting anything you shouldn't. "Oops" isn't an answer the military likes to hear. The government always gets its money back, and military folks can even be prosecuted for over-payments.

The general rule is that spouses lose all military benefits upon divorce. They are no longer dependents. Gone are medical care, ID cards, and access to base exchanges and commissaries.

Strangely enough, a child, even one living with its nonmilitary parent, can still be a dependent, and thus eligible for the military's health-care programs. For that child, the service member can still receive extra money, in the form of additional housing allowances.

But there are gray areas. A spouse from whom a military person is legally separated may qualify for some military benefits but not others. Not all children living with a nonmilitary parent meet the official rules for being a dependent for all purposes, either. When in doubt, talk to a military lawyer.

Lawyers also come into play in divorce proceedings. Courts can give the ex-spouses of military personnel payments known as "alimony" (to support an ex-spouse) or "child support" (obviously, for a child). The government will pay up to 65 percent of a military member's pay directly to an ex-spouse who has a valid court order for alimony or child support. That doesn't require the military person's consent. In fact, it can happen over the active-duty person's objection.

The U.S. military, which is an arm of the federal government, takes seriously orders issued by courts, which are another arm of the government.

Still, the courts aren't all-powerful. Although they can order the military to send some of the money earned by a soldier directly to an ex-spouse, courts cannot order the military to provide free medical care or on-base housing to people who divorce military personnel. Access to those benefits is governed by federal law.

SURVIVOR BENEFITS

Even in peacetime, the military is a dangerous place to be. Between seven hundred and a thousand people die on active duty every year. For those who leave families behind, a wide range of government programs are available.

Monthly Payments

Spouses and dependent children of people who die on active duty can qualify for a monthly payment called "Dependency and Indemnity Compensation," or DIC. The payment is about $850 monthly for a spouse, with more than two hundred dollars extra per month for each child. Those rates increase each year by a few percentage points to keep pace with inflation.

Insurance

The life insurance that's offered to active-duty people is a good deal. It's nearly impossible to match in the private sector, and, unlike private plans, you don't have to worry about the insurer (in this case, the government) trying to find some loophole that will let them wiggle out without paying. Everyone in the military with a family should have Servicemembers' Group Life Insurance (SGLI) at the maximum amount of $200,000 in coverage.

Education Benefits

A program similar to the GI Bill is available to the spouses of people who die on active duty. As happens with the GI Bill, the government limits the kinds of classes it will pay for people to attend. The standard rate

———— ★ ————

He: "A soldier in the right place at the right time
can change the world."

She: "I'd rather hoped you had outgrown that."

—Jackie Willow (D. B. Sweeney) and Rachel Feld
(Mary Stuart Masterson) in *Gardens of Stone*
(Twentieth Century Fox, 1987)

for full-time study is more than four hundred a month. It also increases annually to keep up with inflation.

Home Loans

Surprisingly, the spouses of people who die on active duty can qualify for government-backed home loans under the same GI Bill home-loan program as military folks. Like the program for veterans, this one gives a lot of authority to civilian banks and mortgage companies to decide whether a person can afford to purchase a specific home.

Burial Benefits

There are a variety of programs and benefits designed to help families through the immediate problems arising when someone dies in uniform. The government pays to transport the remains and to purchase a cemetery plot (if necessary). Everyone dying on active duty is eligible for burial in Arlington National Cemetery, regardless of the cause. They are also eligible for burial, free of charge, in any of the 119 national cemeteries maintained by VA officials.

★ ★ 17 ★ ★

YOUR FIRST POSTMILITARY JOB

When boot camp, advanced training and your first unit still lie ahead, it's tough to imagine that one day going in the other direction—leaving the military and returning to the civilian world—might look just as scary. But that day will come. Even Colin Powell, Dwight D. Eisenhower, U. S. Grant, and George Washington had to look for ways of earning a living as a civilian.

When you take off a military uniform for the last time, you'll probably be at least four years older. A spouse and kids may be in your life, or you may be thinking seriously about the idea. The military way of doing things will come naturally to you by then, and the ways of the private sector will seem foreign. Jobs stop looking like a way to pay the bills and begin being stepping stones to a place you want to be five, ten, twenty, forty years in the future.

Getting a good job will be the first order of business after becoming a civilian again, unless you're lucky enough to be able to afford full-time schooling. Fortunately, the military will provide on-the-job experience, formal training, and solid skills that will give you a marketability that you didn't have as a high-school graduate.

On that day in the not-so-distant future, you'll have a lot going for you when you face the civilian world with a new, proud title in your resume—veteran.

FIRST, THE MONEY

Most people leaving active duty have a hefty check from the military in their pockets. That's because the government tries to settle all financial dealings with military folks—what they owe you and what you owe them—on their last day in uniform. Unless arranged differently in advance, the settlement takes the form of a check—not cash and not an electronic transfer of funds.

Here are some of the things affecting that last paycheck.

Salary

Military people are entitled to full pay and benefits until the stroke of midnight of their last day in uniform. (Which also means they're fully covered by military rules and regulations until that moment.)

At a minimum, everyone gets the same, fundamental Basic Pay. If the government hasn't provided you with three meals a day, you'll receive the Basic Allowance for Subsistence (BAS). And if free government housing hasn't been available, then you also receive Basic Allowance for Housing.

Although those payments are usually expressed as monthly rates, they're divided by thirty to create a daily rate when people are discharged before the end of the month.

Leave

People who know they're only going spend a few years in uniform can add substantially to that final paycheck from the military by not using the vacation time—called "leave" by the military—that they earn. They are able to "cash-in" that time by converting unused leave into pay.

When "cashing-in" leave, payments are calculated as one-thirtieth of Basic Pay for each day of unused leave. Other items in the military paycheck, like BAS, BAH, enlistment bonuses and hazardous duty payments, aren't included in calculating unused leave, only Basic Pay.

Everyone earns two and a half days of leave for each month on active duty. There's no credit for partial months. That rate adds up to thirty days per year. Normally, military folks cannot cash in more than sixty days. If you want to try cashing in more than sixty days, discuss your strategy in

———— ☆ ————

"I've been to another planet, Ma!"

—Alex (Lance Guest) in *The Last Starfighter*
(Universal Studios, 1984)

advance with the folks at the finance office. Exceptions are rare, and most involve military commanders prohibiting people from taking leave.

Travel Payments

The military paid to bring you and much of your personal possessions to your first assignment, and then paid to move you and your stuff around the country, perhaps even the world. It's only fitting that the military assumes the cost of getting you back home after discharge.

Travel payments usually include a per diem designed to pay usual costs for food and lodging both for you and for anyone who qualifies as your dependent. The government will either give you an airline, bus, or train ticket, or it will provide a mileage rate—a minimum of fifteen cents per mile—if you drive a private car.

The government will also pay to ship your personal property back home or to store it for a year. There are official limits, which are based upon the pounds authorized for people in each rank. If you're over the limit for your rank, you have to pay the difference.

Most people don't have to travel immediately home after discharge. The government gives most new veterans a year after discharge to move.

These rules about travel payments only involve people leaving active duty with good records who complete the full amount of time they agreed to serve. Those who get in trouble in the military and who are forced out of uniform early may get less generous travel benefits.

Debts

Don't expect the government to forget—or forgive—any debts you owe just because you're leaving. Expect the government to subtract from your final paycheck the full amount for any fines, debts, or other financial obligations.

A debt that many military members don't think about involves enlistment bonuses. If you accepted money to come on active duty for a set time and you don't serve that long, then the government says you owe it money. Serving only two-thirds of your obligated time, for example, means you owe the government for one-third of your bonus.

If you have even the slightest possibility of owing money to the government, don't wait until your last day to deal with the matter. Most of those last-minute crises are resolved in the government's favor. Be smart, have your paperwork in order, and work the system well in advance of your discharge date to answer any questions about owing the government money.

MAKING THE TRANSITION BACK TO CIVILIAN LIFE

Senior folks in the military understand that many active-duty people facing discharge need help and encouragement to make a smooth transition to the civilian workforce. That's why all of the armed forces sponsor a variety of programs to help new veterans find their first civilian jobs. Services available at most military installations include:

Transition Centers

Full-time, trained professionals offer free, one-on-one assistance in job hunting. Many of these services are also offered to the spouses of military personnel. The official names vary among bases.

A typical transition center has books and publications about finding work, with much of the material targeted to specific communities. Most centers also have computer hook-ups into job banks for employers who are looking for military veterans, and a program in which service members post mini-resumes for potential employers to look at.

The Transition Assistance Program

More commonly known as TAP, this free, three-day course is available at many transition centers. TAP is tailored to the needs of new veterans. Run jointly by the Defense Department, the Department of Veterans Affairs (the VA) and the Department of Labor, these TAP classes cover everything the new job seeker needs to know, from writing resumes and putting together job-search networks, to dressing and handling yourself in a job interview.

Unemployment Compensation

U.S. workers who lose their jobs through no fault of their own can claim this. If you leave active duty because you've reached the normal end of your term of service—in other words, if you're not leaving because the military is forcing you out—you probably qualify for unemployment compensation.

Federal law guarantees unemployment compensation to newly discharged veterans. The rules are surprisingly generous. You can collect unemployment compensation wherever you move after taking off your uniform. It doesn't have to be the state where you grew up, the state where

———— ✯ ————

"You're on Rylos, my boy. Stop thinking human.
That's lesson number one."

—Centauri (Robert Preston) in *The Last Starfighter*
(Universal Studios, 1984)

you were discharged, or a state in which you've ever lived. Any state, by federal law, has to give you unemployment compensation.

Rates vary by state. Typically, the program pays about two hundred dollars per week for twenty-six weeks. Recipients must actually look for work while they receive the money, and they must document their efforts.

Unemployment compensation is administered by the states. To find the right office, check a telephone book for the section reserved for numbers of state agencies. Usually, it comes under the state's employment agency.

Networking

As anyone who's done much employment counseling can tell you, networking is what turns most job seekers into former job seekers. Richard Bolles, author of "What Color Is Your Parachute?"—the granddaddy of all books on job hunting—says that about seven out of every ten people looking for work get it through personal contacts. The rest use employment firms, answer newspaper ads, or make mass mailings of their resumes.

The purpose of networking is to find out about jobs before they're advertised in the newspaper or registered with a state employment agency. Useful networking contacts are people in a position to hear about that kind of vacancy. They don't have to be executives or high rollers. Anybody who knows people will do. You, as a soon-to-be-ex-service member, have a ready-made network waiting for you in most communities of this country. It's called the American Legion, the VFW, your old unit's association, or one of the dozens of other nationally based groups representing veterans.

Once you've figured out where you're going to live, check the eligibility rules for those groups and join as many as you can. Attend a few gatherings even if it's not the way you prefer to spend your free time. Let them know who you are and the sorts of work you're looking for. They'll be more than happy to help, for giving veterans a helping hand is what the organized veterans movement is all about.

Time

One of the most helpful—and most precious—tools for anyone looking for work is time. Most experts recommend that military folks begin serious planning and fact-gathering at least eighteen months before their discharge. That's when they should start visiting the nearest transition center, subscribing to the Sunday newspaper for the community where they plan to live, and begin putting together a job-hunting network.

Six months before discharge, people should begin contacting potential employers, visiting communities, and working on resumes. Three months before discharge is when they should start submitting applications and mailing resumes.

If it doesn't interfere with military operations, commanders are supposed to permit active-duty people to take a maximum of ten days for job-hunting. These ten days aren't counted as regular, annual leave. Nor should commanders count as leave the time attending TAP classes and other formal programs at a transition center.

DEMILITARIZING RESUMES AND APPLICATIONS

If you're like millions of other Americans who've worn the uniforms of the U.S. armed forces, you're going to be proud of that association for the rest of your life. Your fellow citizens are grateful for the work you've done for all of us.

Employers take note of young people who've served in the military. That single word, "veteran," on an application shows that someone probably is more mature and has handled greater responsibility than his or her high-school classmates. Supervisors are confident that veterans are drug free, not abusers of alcohol, accustomed to showing up on time and working with others, and conscientious when it comes to following instructions.

But is that enough to get you a job? Nine times out of ten, the supervisor deciding between two equally qualified applicants will hire the veteran.

---------- ☆ ----------

"I can't lose my edge. I've got to keep my strength up. I've got to maintain discipline. Because the hard thing is—I got to get a job."

—Maj. Benson Payne (Damon Wayans) in
Major Payne (Universal Studios, 1994)

But when the choice is between a superbly qualified civilian and an acceptably qualified veteran, guess who gets the job? The civilian.

Here are some of the best pieces of advice I've gathered from conversations with hundreds of veterans and dozens of counselors who specialize in helping military folks find their first civilian jobs. (For more ideas, check my "Drawdown Survival Guide," Naval Institute Press, 1993.)

- Use your DD Form 2586, "Verification of Military Experience and Training." This is a multipage form that's supposed to be given to everyone facing discharge. As the name implies, it itemizes the training and skills that people acquire in the military. That form is a good tool for focusing upon skills. It also identifies the civilian jobs that military folks are qualified for, using something called a "DOT" code. "DOT" stands for *Dictionary of Occupational Titles*, a standard reference that can be found in transition centers, employment centers and even public libraries. A DOT code is a nine-digit number referring to a specific kind of civilian job. By cross-checking your DD Form 2586 with the *Dictionary of Occupational Titles*, veterans can see exactly how civilian employers define jobs. Successful vets tailor their resumes and their applications to the expectations of those civilian employers.

- Completely demilitarize one resume, if only as an experiment. Write a one-page resume that contains a single clue—a line toward the bottom that says something like, "U.S. Army, 1999–2003"—that mentions your military service. Nothing else in the resume should even hint at it.

  If you were a squad leader, write in the resume that you were a supervisor. If you worked on amphibians, write about your skills with small boats and tracked vehicles. If you fixed F-16s, write only about what you can do on any airplane. Force yourself to see your military experience completely through civilian eyes.

  Remember that jobs go to the best qualified. Being a veteran doesn't directly qualify you for anything. The skills and experiences you learned in uniform, however, are priceless. Talk about them with civilian supervisors.

- Of course, rarely will you encounter a situation in which it's to your advantage to submit a completely demilitarized resume. Young people who've put in even a single tour on active duty should especially highlight some features of their military service. It underscores their maturity and dependability. Here are some specific ideas:

  —Do mention that you were in the military, which branch, and the months and years of your service.

  —Don't itemize every assignment.

  —Do mention the highest military decoration you received.

  —Don't list every honor. A supervisor might think you're living in the past.

  —Do mention your rank when you left.

  —Don't itemize every promotion or mention that you were promoted ahead of schedule.

  —Do mention having the Purple Heart.

—Don't mention any award for valor unless applying for a civilian job—law enforcement, firefighter—for which bravery is an issue.

—Do include experiences and skills from civilian jobs before enlisting or while moonlighting in service.

—Don't use military titles, or names of equipment or procedures if there's a perfectly understandable civilian equivalent.

Good jobs don't grow on trees. Nor do they fall into laps—even for deserving veterans.

To get the kind of job you deserve, one that draws on your talents, moves you closer to long-range career goals, and pays the salary you deserve, you'll need to convince a civilian supervisor that you're the best qualified person for the job. Usually, being a veteran comes into hiring decisions only as a tiebreaker.

VETERANS PREFERENCE: FACTS AND A REALITY CHECK

Some employers have formal hiring policies called "veterans preferences." These preferences give most veterans a slight edge over equally qualified nonveterans when hiring decisions are made; disabled veterans may receive a fairly substantial advantage.

Veterans preferences can be confusing. Sometimes, it's important to understand what they're *not*. They're not a guaranteed job, they're not going to put anyone into a job that he or she is unqualified to fill.

Veterans preferences are most commonly found in federal government, state and local government and large corporations. Smaller organizations, where the vast majority of newly discharged veterans find jobs, are less likely to have formal hiring preferences for veterans.

Still, a less formal, unwritten preference is found throughout the private sector. Many people appreciate the importance of military service, and they're willing to give a break to men and women just coming off active

---------- ★ ----------

"You know anything about building?"
"No. But there's one thing I do know. I know how to learn."

—Scrap-boss (Pat Flaherty) and Fred Derry
(Dana Andrews) in *Best Days of Our Lives*
(Samuel Goldwyn, 1946)

duty. After all, many of the people doing the hiring are veterans themselves: they know what you've been through.

Whether or not there is a formal veterans preference program or a soft spot in an old vet's heart for a younger vet who's trying to find a place back in the civilian world, let's not lose sight of the fact that even the best preference is only an advantage, an edge, a break. It's not a polite form of welfare.

Unfortunately, anyone who's done much hiring in the private sector has stories about people who thought their military service meant they were owed a job, even one for which they had no experience. Yes, being responsible for a tank and three crewmen in combat is more demanding than running a fast-food restaurant. But one has no relation to the other. A good fast-food manager is no more likely to make a good tank commander than a good tank commander is guaranteed to be a good fast-food manager.

Those kinds of comparisons don't get anyone on a payroll. If you put your military training to good use and if you learn a few tricks about selling yourself, you will have a better, more direct way of landing a good job. Look at it this way.

In the financial world, the basic unit of measurement is the dollar. In mathematics, it's the number. In dance, it's the movement. But in the job force, where most of us earn the incomes that enable us to meet our basic needs and achieve many dreams, it's the skill.

Skills are what your future boss is looking for. Skills are what the military gave you. Skills are the things to keep in the forefront of your mind—and at the top of your resume—as you make the tricky transition from soldier to civilian.

VETERANS BENEFITS

The uniforms of the U.S. armed forces have an amazing power: they can leave a mark that lasts a lifetime. This mark can be found on every man and woman who has ever sewn on a stripe or pinned on an officer's insignia. All who serve on active duty will carry for their rest of their lives the proud title of "veteran."

In some respects, being a veteran is like being a high school graduate. Once you've earned the title, you have it for the rest of your life. It can't be taken away. But, unlike your academic accomplishments and athletic records, the title of "veteran" is likely to increase in importance to you over the years.

Being a veteran has more than sentimental value. Long before the nation had Social Security, welfare, or unemployment compensation, the government set up special programs for veterans, many of which continue to this day. Home-loan guarantees and financial assistance for schooling are commonly known "perks" of being a veteran.

Those are some of the programs that a grateful nation has established to say "Thank you" to the men and women who choose to spend a few years doing the country's business in uniform. Before you raise your hand and take the oath, you should understand what awaits you a few years down the road, after you hang up your uniform for the last time and reenter the private sector as a veteran.

GI BILL EDUCATION

More people know about the "GI Bill" than can tell you that "GI" stands for "government-issued." The original GI Bill, signed by President Franklin

Roosevelt in 1944, revolutionized post-war America by putting college educations and home ownership within the grasp of ordinary Americans. Educational benefits are still a major reason why young people join the military.

Like all things, the GI Bill has changed in the half-century since its creation. Now called the Montgomery GI Bill, it is less generous than the versions offered to this generation's fathers and grandfathers after Vietnam and World War II. Still, like the original version, it is placing college education—or advanced technical training—within the reach of millions of deserving Americans.

The main difference between the existing GI Bill and the original version is that today's veterans must put some of their own money into the program. The normal rule is that service members who want to take advantage of the program must give up $100 a month from their paychecks for their first year on active duty. It has to be $100 (it can't be less), it has to be done for twelve months (you can't offer $50 for twenty-four months) and it all must begin soon after coming on active duty (you can't delay for a few years).

In return for making that contribution, veterans can receive financial help from the government for advanced schooling, including vocational-technical training. The rates in 1999 were:

- $528 monthly for thirty-six months for people who spent at least three years on active duty.
- $429 monthly for thirty-six months for people who spent less than three years on active duty.
- Up to $700 monthly to people in a hard-to-fill job. We've mentioned these bonuses, called "kickers." If you're eligible for a kicker, you knew it when you enlisted.

These rates can be cut in half for students taking only half the normal load of classes, which doubles the number of months for which payments can be paid. Similar adjustments are made for course loads that are one-quarter and three-quarters of the regular amounts.

You can put your GI Bill money to any purpose you want—paying for classes, buying books, renting an apartment, buying a car, or taking a vacation—but the government will pull the plug if you aren't actually attending classes. The government also reserves the right to approve the institution for which a veteran wants to use GI Bill money. Approval isn't a problem for accredited colleges and universities. This approval process was created to prevent unscrupulous vo-tech institutions from giving veterans useless training.

Schools make it easy for veterans to tap into this benefit. They have the necessary forms; they know the procedure. All you have to do is let them know you intend to use the GI Bill and produce a copy of your discharge paper, the DD Form 214.

Let's repeat two provisions of the GI Bill that are pretty hard-nosed. First, you'll get one chance, early in boot camp, to sign up for the Montgomery GI Bill. If you turn it down, you can't change your mind later and sign up.

A second rule that can seem harsh to some folks is the idea that once the government has withheld $1,200 from your first year's paychecks, you can't get that money back, even if you never sign up for any additional education. It's gone, and you'll never see it again.

GI BILL HOME LOANS

More common than users of GI Bill education benefits are the veterans who use GI Bill benefits to buy their own homes. Since the end of World War II, it's been one of the major perks available to everyone who serves their country honorably in uniform. We've noted that for a major government program, it's surprisingly decentralized. You pick the home. You pick the mortgage company. You negotiate the sales price. The government steps in only if things are getting out of hand.

Although everyone refers to the program as the GI Bill home loan, that's not a good description of the program. The government doesn't loan money to anyone. The government's role is to promise the mortgage company that if you don't pay the mortgage, Uncle Sam will step up and pay those bills.

Because Uncle Sam guarantees the loan, loan companies know that veterans with GI Bill benefits are less risky that other homebuyers. Peace of mind for the loan officer translates into a better deal for the veteran.

Since the basic transaction is between the veteran and the loan company (with the government hovering in the wings like a financial guardian angel), the loan company has a say in this benefit. The loan company, using standard industry yardsticks, will decide whether you can afford to buy a

———— ☆ ————

"This is the VA, soldier. The enemy is behind those desks."

—Luther Jerome (Keith David) in *Article 99*
(Orion Pictures, 1992)

$100,000 home, a $200,000 home or a $15,000 trailer. A GI Bill home loan isn't going to let you buy a house that a mortgage company says you can't afford.

Unlike the educational version of the GI Bill, under the home loan program there are no deadlines for using your benefit. You can use it to buy a home immediately after leaving the military or sixty years later. You can even use it to buy more than one home, but only one home at a time. One of the few restrictions the government imposes upon veterans is that it must be a home in which the veteran lives. You can't use your GI Bill home-loan benefit to buy a nice place for your mother, at least, not if you plan to live elsewhere.

First-time homeowners are especially fond of one feature: usually, they don't have to make a down payment under the GI Bill to buy a home. Down payments are the rule for most purchases for civilians. As a practical matter, though, most veterans will have to pay immediately some of the costs ("points") of buying a home. That can range from several hundred dollars to a couple thousand dollars.

As with GI Bill educational benefits, veterans don't have to worry about knowing which form to submit to which office. Your real estate agent knows exactly what to do. After all, the real estate agent doesn't get paid until your loan is approved.

Although the GI Bill home loans have been around since World War II and all veterans have the same benefit, the eligibility rules have been fiddled with over the years. Your father and grandfather may have had to serve longer, or shorter, periods on active duty to qualify. Find out what exact rules apply to you as soon as you begin thinking seriously about buying a home.

The people who administer your GI Bill benefits are in the U.S. Department of Veterans Affairs. If you think you're being treated unfairly by a real estate agent, a mortgage company, or a home seller, the folks at the VA want to know about it. Contact your nearest VA office. You'll find them in the blue pages of the telephone book under "U.S. Government."

———— ★ ————

"I'm not the kind of man to take 'No answer' for an answer."

—Col. Purdy (Paul Ford) in
The Teahouse of the August Moon (MGM, 1956)

MEDICAL CARE

Leaving the military means walking away from a home, a job, many friends, a regular paycheck and a way of life. It also means leaving behind something else that some people consider more important than everything else—a doctor.

Fortunately, your military service will entitle you to some medical care after you leave the government's payroll. Here are some of the major health-care programs.

Life-long Medical Care

Most veterans retain only a few short-term medical benefits after their discharges. We'll look at those benefits below. But other veterans might be eligible for life-long medical care in hospitals and clinics operated by the VA.

These are veterans who have illnesses, injuries, or diseases that they can connect to their military service. It may be the broken leg that hasn't been right since an accident on maneuvers. Or it could be the cancer that was detected on active duty.

You don't have to have a medical problem that was caused by your official duties—just something that began or worsened during your stint on active duty.

Physical Examination

Many military folks on their way out the main gate for the last time tend to cut corners at the base hospital. By regulation, they're supposed to receive a final physical examination that's as comprehensive as the one they received coming in.

Military doctors, who are overworked taking care of sick people, might not want to spend a lot of time with a healthy, soon-to-be-ex-patient. Many military members don't want the hassles of being poked, prodded, and told to perform some very private bodily functions.

So it's perfectly natural to want to skip the last physical. Fight the temptation. For many people, it's the last time they'll see a doctor for a long time. Some day, perhaps decades from now, you may want to prove that a specific medical problem began in the service. That's easy to do if you've had a comprehensive, final physical that documents your health and your problems as you were leaving the military.

Transition Medical Care

These days most people receive their health care through employer-sponsored plans. Veterans and their families can find themselves without medical insurance if a civilian job isn't waiting for them immediately after discharge.

Since the early 1990s, the military has offered a health insurance plan designed to fill those gaps in coverage. Called the Continued Health Care Benefit Program, it is purchased in three-month blocks, with eighteen months the longest it can be held.

It's not cheap, but then again, neither are medical bills. In 1999, three months' coverage cost $993 for an individual and $1,996 for a family. Generally, participants pay the first $500 in yearly medical expenses, and the plan picks up 80 percent of the rest.

Keep in mind that many employer-sponsored insurance plans don't offer immediate coverage to new employees. Many more have periods for which they won't cover preexisting medical conditions. Despite the costs, the military's transitional health insurance makes sense for many new veterans, especially those with families.

Dental Care

The last thing that many people worry about as they're coming to the end of their time on active duty is their teeth. They tend to skip their last dental appointments. Then, once they're civilians again, they find themselves delaying visits even longer, because of unemployment or out-of-pocket costs from employer-provided plans.

Fortunately, a little-known provision is on the books that allows newly discharged veterans to receive free medical care in VA clinics for up to 180 days after leaving the military. Recipients don't have to go through the normal red tape surrounding most VA medical benefits. A copy of your

———— ☆ ————

"We can't have you wandering around out there
wasting friendly civilians."

—Col. Samuel Trautman (Richard Crenna) to
John Rambo (Sylvester Stallone) in *First Blood*
(Artisan Entertainment, 1982)

discharge papers and, if possible, your military dental records are all you need to schedule an appointment with a VA dentist.

Usually, it's a one-time deal. The dentists will get as much done as they can in a single session. The result might be more dental work than you're comfortable with. But it's first-rate dentistry, and you can't beat the price.

Records

All of your personnel, medical, and dental records are kept by the government after a veteran's discharge. Folks who are about to leave the military should make copies of those records to take with them.

LIFE INSURANCE

Life insurance is a way for breadwinners to ensure that if they die, the people who depend upon them financially will have an income. It's a "must" for people with families, with parents who depend upon them or with brothers and sisters they're helping to raise. Fortunately, a low-cost, government-backed life insurance program is available to people leaving active duty.

It's called "Veterans' Group Life Insurance," or VGLI. It's not free. No one's going to tell you what to do to get it. You must take the time to understand the rules and figure out if getting this insurance makes financial sense for you. But, especially for veterans with families, the time and the cost are well worth it. Here are some highlights:

Eligibility

Almost everyone leaving active duty can sign up for veterans life insurance. Among the few who cannot are those who didn't take the active-duty life insurance—Servicemembers' Group Life Insurance, or SGLI—and people discharged because they got in serious trouble.

Signing up has to be done within a year of leaving the military. Within that year, another deadline is important: if you sign up for VGLI within 120 days of leaving active duty, you can get the coverage simply by paying the first month's premium. A physical examination may be necessary to join between the 121st day after discharge and the first anniversary. If you haven't taken VGLI by your first anniversary, the only way to get it is to come back in uniform and start all over again.

Duration

VGLI coverage is known as "term" insurance. That means that the coverage lasts for a specific time—or term. In this case, the term is five years. At the end of that period, recipients can renew for another five years.

Until 1993, VGLI coverage couldn't be renewed at the end of the first five-year term. Now, veterans can keep it for their entire lives.

Amounts

"Coverage" is the amount of insurance money that your family would receive if you die. For VGLI, the coverage can range from $10,000 to $200,000. Every veteran can purchase at least $100,000 in coverage. For coverage between $100,000 and $200,000, veterans are limited to the amounts that they purchased for the SGLI active-duty insurance.

Rates

Like all life insurance programs, you have to make a monthly payment, a premium, to receive coverage. The rates are set by age and the amount of coverage you want to purchase.

For people aged twenty-nine and younger, the rate for ten thousand dollars in coverage during the year 2000 was less than two dollars per month. Each additional ten thousand in coverage costs less than two dollars more per month.

Beneficiary

A "beneficiary" is the person to whom the insurance money is paid if you die. VGLI recipients can make anyone their beneficiaries. It doesn't have to be a relative. In fact, it doesn't even have to be a person. The beneficiary can be a company, the veteran's estate, or any legal entity.

To minimize the chance of legal complications, veterans should record the names of their beneficiaries on forms provided by the office running the program.

★ ★ 19 ★ ★

SPECIAL VETS,
SPECIAL PROBLEMS

"Veteran" is a title which all men and women who serve their country in uniform carry for the rest of their lives. For some, it means more than others. For a few, the reminder is more than sentimental. The tools of military service—tanks, heavy shipboard equipment, jets—are dangerous, and people leave the military every day with physical problems that require lifetime care.

Since the Revolutionary War, the people of the United States have taken care of those with problems caused by military service. During colonial days, many of those programs were informal and the responsibility of communities. Since the Civil War, they've become more formal and the province of the federal government.

Taking care of veterans is so important that the secretary of the VA is a member of the cabinet, overseeing one of the fourteen major departments in the executive branch of government.

Unfortunately, as veterans programs moved away from communities and into the federal government, everything became more complex. No law says, simply, "Take care of sick vets." Instead, many laws spell out the exact categories of sick vets—often, even how much of which symptoms they must have—in order to qualify for federal benefits.

If the following chapter sounds in places as if we're quoting from a law book, it's because we are looking at programs that are based upon federal law, where small words can have huge importance. But take heart. None of this is beyond the understanding of a high school graduate who takes the time to see exactly how the legal lines are drawn.

CHRONIC MEDICAL PROBLEMS

All military veterans who leave active duty with a medical problem may qualify for free medical care for their rest of their lives, plus a monthly payment called "VA disability compensation.'

The problem doesn't have to be one that was directly related to their military duties. The law books say it must be "incurred or aggravated" during service, which means it happened between enlistment and discharge.

As far as the VA is concerned, there's no difference between the veteran with a leg broken by shrapnel in combat that didn't heal properly and the veteran with a leg that still gives him trouble after sliding into second base during an off-duty softball game. Both receive the same medical care, with the same priority, and, if the situation warrants, a monthly disability check.

Getting Treated

It's only fair that if something happens during active duty that causes continuing health problems, the government should provide medical care for as long as you need it. That's exactly what happens for veterans.

But let's look for a moment at the other side of that idea. It's not fair for the U.S. taxpayer to pay your medical bills if your problems have nothing to do with your military service. In fact, the VA would rapidly use up its medical budget if each of the twenty-six million veterans in the United States could walk into a VA hospital, say, "I've got a problem that was caused by my military service" and receive free treatment.

The VA does what you'd probably do if you were in charge. VA officials have set up a formal review process that looks at each veteran who believes he or she has health problems that came about while wearing the uniform. During that review, the veteran undergoes physical examinations. The vet's military medical record is examined, and the veteran gets the chance to put forward the best arguments for getting coverage.

If VA officials agree with the veteran during that review, which can take months, they will announce that the medical problem is "service con-

──────── ☆ ────────

"You're home now, kid."

—Al Stephenson (Frederic March) in
Best Days of Our Lives (Samuel Goldwyn, 1946)

nected," and a percentage figure will be attached to the problem. For example, the vet will be described as being "20 percent disabled" or "90 percent disabled." The percentage is always divisible by ten.

Once people have an official percentage attached to a medical problem and the words "service connected" in their VA medical records, they can be treated at any VA hospital in the country. They can receive drugs and rehabilitative therapy. If a medical problem can't be cured, then veterans will receive that free medical care for the rest of their lives.

Monthly Payments

Medical problems often cause more than physical problems. They also cause financial hardship.

For decades, the government has offered monthly payments to veterans with service-connected health problems that interfere with their ability to earn a living. Called "VA disability compensation," it's a monthly payment designed to give sick and injured veterans a little extra money.

Getting VA disability compensation isn't as difficult as you might guess. The first step is undergoing the reviews that are needed to be authorized VA medical care. The stamp of "service connected" in a veteran's medical file means that, automatically, that vet will be considered for disability payments.

The percentage figure assigned to the medical problem determines how much people receive every month in disability pay. Here are the rates in effect for 1999:

10 percent	$96
20 percent	184
30 percent	282
40 percent	404
50 percent	576
60 percent	726
70 percent	916
80 percent	1,062
90 percent	1,196
100 percent	1,989

That money isn't taxed. It isn't decreased if a recipient is able to earn an income. No one looks over the shoulders of veterans to see how they spend it. It's theirs. They earned it.

PENSION FOR COMBAT VETERANS

Everyone has a job to do in the military, and most people have little say about what they do or where they go. That's one reason why veterans' benefits are the same for everyone, without distinction for the job you did, where you served, or when you wore the uniform.

One benefit, however, is different in its eligibility rules: only folks who served on active duty during wartime can apply. It's called a "VA Pension."

This benefit is for wartime veterans who have no income. The pension isn't large, and it shrinks by one dollar for each dollar of income a veteran receives. But it ensures that health care and some money go to people who served their country when there were real risks in wearing a uniform.

Who Gets It

As with many VA benefits, the rules can be painfully exacting. Individual words can rule in—or out—thousands of people from the program.

Pension recipients must have served during wartime. Congress decides which conflicts are covered. So far, the list includes both world wars, Korea, Vietnam, and the Gulf War, but not such actions as Somalia, Haiti, Panama, or Bosnia. To be eligible, veterans didn't have to be in combat; they don't even have to have been overseas. But they did have to be on active duty during that official period of conflict.

The veteran must have a discharge that's officially called—and this is another finely split legal hair—"under other than dishonorable conditions." The veteran cannot have medical problems linked to alcoholism, drug abuse, or venereal disease. (A good legal adviser, however, knows ways around all of these disqualifiers.)

Finally, the veteran must have some medical problem that is permanent and totally disabling. That problem must be unrelated to anything that happened while on active duty. Or, put another way, the veteran must have a severe disability that's not service connected.

What They Get

Like veterans with service-related medical problems, recipients of VA pensions are eligible for free, lifetime medical care for their problems. The care is usually given at hospitals and clinics run by the VA. If the care is to be provided somewhere else, the VA—not the veteran—decides where.

——————— ☆ ———————

"All I've ever wanted is to be treated like everyone else."
—Homer Parrish (Harold Russell) in
Best Days of Our Lives (Samuel Goldwyn, 1946)

———————————————

It shouldn't strike anyone as unfair that people with VA pensions are taken care of after the veterans with service-connected needs. It doesn't mean that pension vets are turned away; it may mean that they may have to wait a little longer or schedule appointments at inconvenient times.

Still, like the folks receiving VA disability pay, the pension recipients qualify for a full range of medical care, from pharmacies and medical supplies to hospitalizations and, if warranted, long-term care.

Although the medical care is the most important benefit for most pension recipients, there also is a monthly paycheck. Several inflexible strings are attached to the pension checks. Recipients have to be honest with VA officials about their property and their income. If the total value of their property rises above a certain level—usually around $30,000—they can't receive a pension. Also, one dollar is taken from their pension checks for each dollar they receive in outside income.

Here are the rates in effect in 1999 for VA pensions. Note that the financial obligations of veterans have nothing to do with the amounts. The only factor affecting rates is the number of people in the veteran's household:

Veteran without family	$8,788
Veteran with one family member	11,497
Housebound veteran	10,729
Housebound vet with family	13,448
Vet unable to care for self	14,647
Vet unable to care, with family	17,365

As anyone who has paid bills for a while can tell you, this money is barely enough to keep a roof over your head and food on the table.

LEAVING THE MILITARY WITH PROBLEMS

The military isn't just a job. It's a complete society, where there are expectations and rules that don't have anything to do with your ability to be an asset to a civilian employer.

The vast majority of people who have served their country in uniform have no problem living under the military's rules, but there always are some who leave active duty with problems in their records.

Maybe they still needed to learn some lessons about handling responsibility and living with other people. Others found themselves making decisions for the first time in their lives . . . and they made bad choices. Some had their first experiences with alcohol or illegal drugs and discovered that they liked that stuff too much.

Unfortunately, all of those situations can result in people leaving the armed forces in ways that prevent them from receiving veterans benefits, from getting a security clearance, or joining the federal civil service. Many civilian employers will even refuse to hire people with bad military records.

But there is good news for people who run into problems with the military. The government knows that good people leave the armed forces every year for reasons that shouldn't haunt them for the rest of their lives. Programs have been created to help veterans in those pickles.

Problem Discharges

When people leave active duty (or the reserves) for good, they are "discharged." They receive a DD Form 214, "discharge papers."

The discharge papers show where you've served, what you've done, which awards you've received. They also say whether you did a good job in uniform, a bad job or something in between. That's the thing that can cause problems later. If your discharge papers say you got into serious trouble in the military—or, more technically, if you get a "dishonorable discharge"—that can have far-reaching effects with private-sector jobs.

Fortunately, all of the services have boards that do nothing but examine the discharges of former service members and see if the veterans should be issued a better discharge.

Those boards are called "Discharge Review Boards." Veterans must request them to examine a particular discharge. The boards don't automatically examine all discharges. Major veterans groups, military lawyers, and VA offices have the paperwork necessary to begin a formal reexamination of a discharge. Also, check the VA's homepage, http://www.va.gov. You may be able to download the proper form, DD Form 293, "Application for Review of Discharge or Dismissal."

A second kind of panel, a "Board for the Correction of Military Records," can review discharges and take other actions, such as ordering promotions, changing evaluations, or bringing veterans back on active duty.

Again, VA offices, military lawyers and major veterans groups have the necessary forms. Or you might find it on the VA's homepage, http://www.va.gov. It's DD Form 149, "Application for Correction of Military or Naval Record."

Records: The ticket of admission for many VA programs are your discharge papers. Every veteran should have a several copies of his or her DD Form 214, and they should be in a place where family members know where they are and can get them in an emergency. Safety deposit boxes at a bank are a good idea, but only if other people have access to the box. Copies of discharge papers can be obtained by writing to: National Personnel Records Center, Military Personnel Records, 9700 Page Boulevard, St. Louis, MO 63132.

Requests should be typed or printed clearly. They should include the veteran's full name, birth date, branch of service, Social Security number, and dates of service. Requests can be made in letters, but for fast results people should use Standard Form 180, "Request Pertaining to Military Records." That form is obtainable from VA offices, military lawyers, major veterans organizations, and the VA's homepage, http://www.va.gov.

FINAL HONORS

Nothing sets veterans apart from other civilians like the fact that they are entitled to distinctive funerals and burials in special cemeteries. You don't have to be a highly decorated hero or a military careerist.

Many communities have "national cemeteries," which are owned and operated by the VA. Only veterans and their immediate families can be buried there. As a general rule, anyone who has served on active duty can be buried in a national cemetery.

The most famous veteran's cemetery is Arlington National Cemetery outside Washington, D.C. Because space is restricted at Arlington, its eligibility rules are tighter. Burial there is limited to retired military, recipients of the Purple Heart and the highest decorations for valor, POWs, and severely disabled veterans.

———— ★ ————

"May the luck of the Seven Pillars of Gooluu be with you at all times."

—Centauri (Robert Preston) to young recruits in
The Last Starfighter (Universal Studios, 1984)

The remains of any veteran with an honorable discharge can be buried at sea by the Navy. Families are rarely present for these burials, which are performed during military missions.

Veterans buried in private cemeteries are usually eligible for a headstone or marker from the government.

Military honor guards to escort veterans to their final resting places have become iffy, as the military has shrunk since the end of the Cold War. But, by law, the military has to send at least two uniformed representatives to the burial of any veteran whose family requests their presence.

Local funeral directors have the latest information about burial at national cemeteries, at sea, and the availability of honor guards.

★ ★ Appendix A ★ ★

THE MILITARY CREDO

Military service has been a higher calling, almost a priesthood, to some of history's greatest leaders. No one captured that spirit more eloquently that General Douglas MacArthur in a speech to the cadets of the U.S. Military Academy at West Point on May 12, 1962.

MacArthur was one of the nation's few five-star leaders during World War II, when he commanded allied forces in the Southwest Pacific. He was awarded the Medal of Honor for his stubborn defense of the Philippines earlier in the war. His father, Arthur MacArthur, was also an Army general and Medal of Honor recipient.

A West Point graduate and later the academy's superintendent, Mac-Arthur fashioned the speech around the West Point motto, "Duty, Honor, Country," when he accepted, late in life, an award from the school.

The general died two years later, on April 5, 1964. He is buried in Norfolk, Virginia. Here is the text of that famous speech:

> As I was leaving the hotel this morning, a doorman asked me, "Where are you headed for, General?" And when I replied, "West Point," he remarked, "Beautiful place. Have you ever been there before?"
>
> No human being could fail to be deeply moved by such a tribute as this [award you have given me today]. Coming from a profession I have served so long and a people I have loved so well, it fills me with an emotion I cannot express.
>
> But this award is not intended primarily to honor a personality, but to symbolize a great moral code—a code of conduct and

chivalry of those who guard this beloved land of culture and ancient descent. For all hours and for all time, it is an expression of the ethics of the American soldier. That I should be integrated in this way with so noble an ideal arouses a sense of pride, and yet of humility, which will be with me always.

Duty, honor, country: Those three hallowed words reverently dictate what you ought to be, what you can be, what you will be. They are your rallying point to build courage when courage seems to fail, to regain faith when there seems to be little cause for faith, to create hope when hope becomes forlorn.

Unhappily, I possess neither that eloquence of diction, that poetry of imagination, nor that brilliance of metaphor to tell you all that they mean. The unbelievers will say they are but words, but a slogan, but a flamboyant phrase. Every pedant, every demagogue, every cynic, every hypocrite, every troublemaker, and, I am sorry to say, some others of an entirely different character, will try to downgrade them even to the extent of mockery and ridicule.

But these are some of the things they do. They build your basic character. They mold you for your future roles as the custodians of the Nation's defense. They make you strong enough to know when you are weak, and brave enough to face yourself when you are afraid.

They teach you to be proud and unbending in honest failure, but humble and gentle in success; not to substitute words for actions, not to seek the path of comfort, but to face the stress and spur of difficulty and challenge; to learn to stand up in the storm, but to have compassion on those who fall; to master yourself before you seek to master others; to have a heart that is clean, a goal that is high; to learn to laugh, yet never forget how to weep; to reach into the future, yet never neglect the past; to be serious, yet never to take yourself too seriously; to be modest so that you will remember the simplicity of true greatness, the open mind of true wisdom, the meekness of true strength.

They give you a temperate will, a quality of the imagination, a vigor of the emotions, a freshness of the deep springs of life, a temperamental predominance of courage over timidity, of an appetite for adventure over love of ease. They create in your heart the sense of wonder, the unfailing hope of what next, and joy and inspiration of life. They teach you in this way to be an officer and a gentleman.

And what sort of soldiers are those you are to lead? Are they reliable? Are they brave? Are they capable of victory? Their story is known to all of you. It is the story of the American man-at-arms. My estimate of him was formed on the battlefield many, many years ago, and has never changed.

I regarded him then, as I regard him now, as one of the world's noblest figures; not only as one of the finest military characters, but also as one of the most stainless. His name and fame are the birthright of every American citizen. In his youth and strength, his love and loyalty, he gave all that mortality can give. He needs no eulogy from me or from any other man. He has written his own history and written it in red on his enemy's breast.

But when I think of his patience in adversity, of his courage under fire and of his modesty in victory, I am filled with an emotion of admiration I cannot put into words. He belongs to history as furnishing one of the greatest examples of successful patriotism. He belongs to posterity as the instructor of future generations in the principles of liberty and freedom. He belongs to the present, to us, by his virtues and by his achievements.

In twenty campaigns, on a hundred battlefields, around a thousand campfires, I have witnessed that enduring fortitude, that patriotic self-abnegation, and that invincible determination which have carved his statue in the hearts of his people. From one end of the world to the other, he has drained deep the chalice of courage.

As I listened to those songs [of the West Point glee club], in memory's eye I could see those staggering columns of the First World War, bending under soggy packs on many a weary march, from dripping dusk to drizzling dawn, slogging ankle deep through the mire of shell-pocked roads to form grimly for the attack, blue-lipped, covered with sludge and mud, chilled by the wind and rain, driving home to their objective, and for many to the judgment seat of God.

I do not know the dignity of their birth, but I do know the glory of their death. They died, unquestioning, uncomplaining, with faith in their hearts, and on their lips the hope that we would go on to victory. Always for them: Duty, honor, country. Always their blood, and sweat, and tears, as we sought the way and the light and the truth.

And twenty years after, on the other side of the globe, again the filth of murky foxholes, the stench of ghostly trenches, the slime of dripping dugouts, those boiling suns of relentless heat, those torrential rains of devastating storms, the loneliness and utter desolation of jungle trails, the bitterness of long separation from those they loved and cherished, the deadly pestilence of tropical disease, the horror of stricken areas of war.

Their resolute and determined defense, their swift and sure attack, their indomitable purpose, their complete and decisive victory—always through the bloody haze of their last reverberating shot, the vision of gaunt, ghastly men, reverently following your password of duty, honor, country.

The code which those words perpetuate embraces the highest moral law and will stand the test of any ethics or philosophies ever promulgated for the uplift of mankind. Its requirements are for the things that are right and its restraints are from the things that are wrong.

The soldier, above all other men, is required to practice the greatest act of religious training—sacrifice. In battle, and in the face of danger and death, he discloses those divine attributes which his Maker gave when He created man in His own image. No physical courage and no greater strength can take the place of the divine help which alone can sustain him. However hard the incidents of war may be, the soldier who is called upon to offer and to give his life for his country is the noblest development of mankind.

You now face a new world, a world of change. The thrust into outer space of the satellite, spheres, and missiles marks a beginning of another epoch in the long story of mankind. In the five or more billions of years the scientists tell us it has taken to form the earth, in the three or more million years of development of the human race, there has never been a more abrupt or staggering evolution.

We deal now, not with things of this world alone, but with the illimitable distances and as yet unfathomed mysteries of the universe. We are reaching out for a new and boundless frontier.

We speak in strange terms of harnessing the cosmic energy, of making winds and tides work for us, of creating unheard of synthetic materials to supplement or even replace our old standard basics; to purify sea water for our drink; of mining ocean floors for new fields of wealth and food; of disease preventatives to expand life into the hundred of years; of controlling the weather for a more equitable distribution of heat and cold, of rain and shine; of spaceships to the moon; of the primary target in war, no longer limited to the armed forces of an enemy, but instead to include his civil populations; of ultimate conflict between a united human race and the sinister forces of some other planetary galaxy; of such dreams and fantasies as to make life the most exciting of all times.

And through all this welter of change and development your mission remains fixed, determined, inviolable. It is to win our wars. Everything else in your professional career is but corollary to this vital dedication. All other public purposes, all other public projects, all other public needs, great or small, will find others for their accomplishment; but you are the ones who are trained to fight.

Yours is the profession of arms, the will to win, the sure knowledge that in war there is no substitute for victory, that if you lose, the Nation will be destroyed, that the very obsession of your public service must be duty, honor, country.

Others will debate the controversial issues, national and international, which divide men's minds. But serene, calm, aloof, you stand as the nation's war guardian, as its lifeguard from the raging tides of international conflict, as its gladiator in the arena of battle. For a century and a half you have defended, guarded, and protected its hallowed traditions of liberty and freedom, of right and justice.

Let civilian voices argue the merits or demerits of our processes of government: Whether our strength is being sapped by deficit financing indulged in too long, by federal paternalism grown too mighty, by power groups grown too arrogant, by politics grown too corrupt, by crime grown too rampant, by morals grown too low, by taxes grown too high, by extremists grown too violent; whether our personal liberties are as thorough and complete as they should be.

These great national problems are not for your professional participation or military solution. Your guidepost stands out like a tenfold beacon in the night: Duty, honor, country.

You are the leaven which binds together the entire fabric of our national system of defense. From your ranks come the great captains who hold the Nation's destiny in their hands the moment the war tocsin sounds. The long, gray line has never failed us. Were you to do so, a million ghosts in olive drab, in brown khaki, in blue and gray, would rise from their white crosses, thundering those magic words: Duty, honor, country.

This does not mean that you are warmongers. On the contrary, the soldier above all other people prays for peace, for he must suffer and bear the deepest wounds and scars of war. But always in our ears ring the ominous words of Plato, that wisest of all philosophers: "Only the dead have seen the end of war."

The shadows are lengthening for me. The twilight is here. My days of old have vanished—tone and tint. They have gone glimmering through the dreams of things that were. Their memory is one of wondrous beauty, watered by tears and coaxed and caressed by the smiles of yesterday. I listen vainly, but with thirsty ear, for the witching melody of faint bugles blowing reveille, of far drums beating the long roll.

In my dreams I hear again the crash of guns, the rattle of musketry, the strange, mournful mutter of the battlefield. But in the evening of my memory always I come back to West Point. Always there echoes and re-echoes: Duty, honor, country.

Today marks my final roll call with you. But I want you to know that when I cross the river, my last conscious thoughts will be of the corps, and the corps, and the corps. I bid you farewell.

✶ ✶ Appendix B ✶ ✶

TEN RIBBONS TO RECOGNIZE

	Army	Navy	Air Force	Marine Corps	Coast Guard
Medal of Honor: *Top award for combat valor*	Light Blue	Light Blue	Light Blue	Light Blue	Light Blue
Second highest Award for combat bravery	Distinguished Service Cross	Navy Cross Dark blue	Air Force Cross: gray center	Navy Cross Dark blue	Navy Cross Dark blue
Silver Star: *Third highest combat award*	Red center white,blue	Red center white,blue	Red center white,blue	Red center white,blue	Red center white,blue
Highest award for non-combat bravery	Soldiers Medal *Red and white*	Navy and Marine Corps Medal	Airman's Medal, *gold& blue*	Navy and Marine Corps Medal	Coast Guard Medal, *red & white*
Purple Heart: *Wounded in combat*	Bright purple	Bright purple	Bright purple	Bright purple	Bright purple
POW Medal	Black with red border	Black with red border	Black with red border	Black with red border	Black with red border
Vietnam Service Medal: *In combat zone for war*	Wide gold stripes	Wide gold stripes	Wide gold stripes	Wide gold stripes	Wide gold stripes
SW Asia Service Medal: *In Middle East for war*	Wide tan stripes	Wide tan stripes	Wide tan stripes	Wide tan stripes	Wide tan stripes
Armed Forces Expeditionary Medal: *Other combat situations*	Wide light blue	Wide light blue	Wide light blue	Wide light blue	Wide light blue
Good Conduct Medal	Red center	Red	White	Red, blue center	Red, white center

✯ ✯ Appendix C ✯ ✯

RANK INSIGNIA

U.S. Army

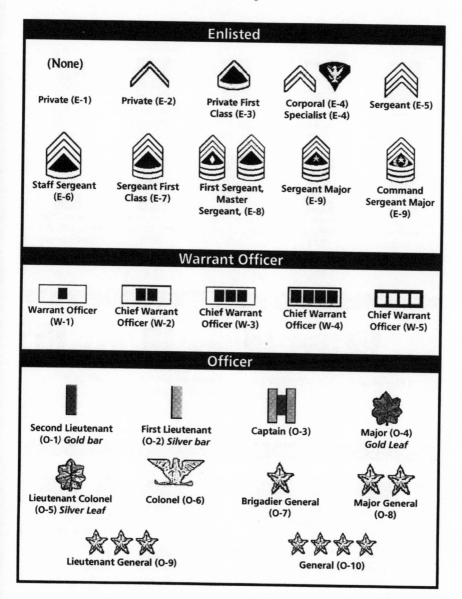

Enlisted

(None)
Private (E-1)

Private (E-2)

Private First Class (E-3)

Corporal (E-4)
Specialist (E-4)

Sergeant (E-5)

Staff Sergeant (E-6)

Sergeant First Class (E-7)

First Sergeant, Master Sergeant, (E-8)

Sergeant Major (E-9)

Command Sergeant Major (E-9)

Warrant Officer

Warrant Officer (W-1)

Chief Warrant Officer (W-2)

Chief Warrant Officer (W-3)

Chief Warrant Officer (W-4)

Chief Warrant Officer (W-5)

Officer

Second Lieutenant (O-1) *Gold bar*

First Lieutenant (O-2) *Silver bar*

Captain (O-3)

Major (O-4) *Gold Leaf*

Lieutenant Colonel (O-5) *Silver Leaf*

Colonel (O-6)

Brigadier General (O-7)

Major General (O-8)

Lieutenant General (O-9)

General (O-10)

Navy and Coast Guard

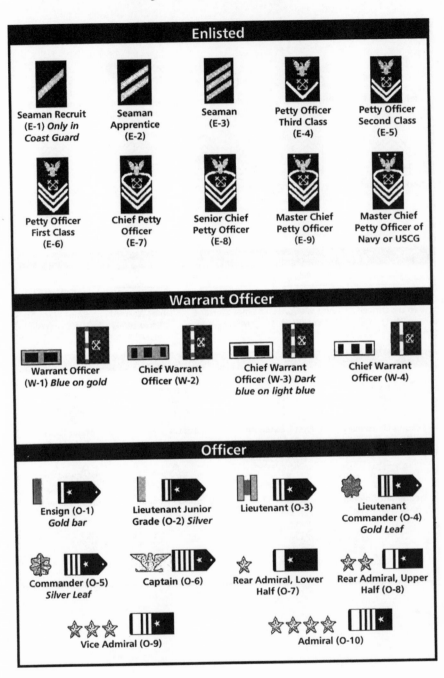

Enlisted

Seaman Recruit (E-1) *Only in Coast Guard*

Seaman Apprentice (E-2)

Seaman (E-3)

Petty Officer Third Class (E-4)

Petty Officer Second Class (E-5)

Petty Officer First Class (E-6)

Chief Petty Officer (E-7)

Senior Chief Petty Officer (E-8)

Master Chief Petty Officer (E-9)

Master Chief Petty Officer of Navy or USCG

Warrant Officer

Warrant Officer (W-1) *Blue on gold*

Chief Warrant Officer (W-2)

Chief Warrant Officer (W-3) *Dark blue on light blue*

Chief Warrant Officer (W-4)

Officer

Ensign (O-1) *Gold bar*

Lieutenant Junior Grade (O-2) *Silver*

Lieutenant (O-3)

Lieutenant Commander (O-4) *Gold Leaf*

Commander (O-5) *Silver Leaf*

Captain (O-6)

Rear Admiral, Lower Half (O-7)

Rear Admiral, Upper Half (O-8)

Vice Admiral (O-9)

Admiral (O-10)

U.S. Air Force

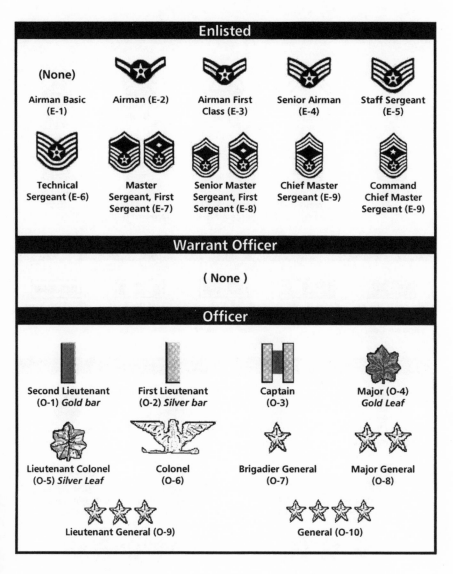

Enlisted

(None)
Airman Basic (E-1)

Airman (E-2)

Airman First Class (E-3)

Senior Airman (E-4)

Staff Sergeant (E-5)

Technical Sergeant (E-6)

Master Sergeant, First Sergeant (E-7)

Senior Master Sergeant, First Sergeant (E-8)

Chief Master Sergeant (E-9)

Command Chief Master Sergeant (E-9)

Warrant Officer

(None)

Officer

Second Lieutenant (O-1) *Gold bar*

First Lieutenant (O-2) *Silver bar*

Captain (O-3)

Major (O-4) *Gold Leaf*

Lieutenant Colonel (O-5) *Silver Leaf*

Colonel (O-6)

Brigadier General (O-7)

Major General (O-8)

Lieutenant General (O-9)

General (O-10)

U.S. Marine Corps

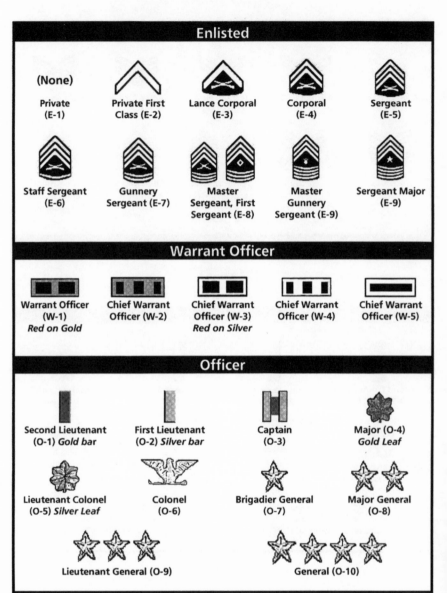

Enlisted

(None)
Private
(E-1)

Private First
Class (E-2)

Lance Corporal
(E-3)

Corporal
(E-4)

Sergeant
(E-5)

Staff Sergeant
(E-6)

Gunnery
Sergeant (E-7)

Master
Sergeant, First
Sergeant (E-8)

Master
Gunnery
Sergeant (E-9)

Sergeant Major
(E-9)

Warrant Officer

Warrant Officer
(W-1)
Red on Gold

Chief Warrant
Officer (W-2)

Chief Warrant
Officer (W-3)
Red on Silver

Chief Warrant
Officer (W-4)

Chief Warrant
Officer (W-5)

Officer

Second Lieutenant
(O-1) *Gold bar*

First Lieutenant
(O-2) *Silver bar*

Captain
(O-3)

Major (O-4)
Gold Leaf

Lieutenant Colonel
(O-5) *Silver Leaf*

Colonel
(O-6)

Brigadier General
(O-7)

Major General
(O-8)

Lieutenant General (O-9)

General (O-10)

✯ ✯ Appendix D ✯ ✯

SHORT HISTORIES OF THE MILITARY SERVICES

ARMY

A history of the U.S. Army is a history of the United States. Many of the nation's greatest events involved its ground forces. The early exploration of the continent and a multitude of scientific developments are owed to this branch of the military. The army was also a testing ground for many of the nation's political leaders.

In a formal sense, the U.S. Army is older than the nation. Its birthday is June 14, 1775—nearly thirteen months before the Declaration of Independence—when the Continental Congress assumed control of a collection of New England militia units and authorized creation of ten new companies of riflemen.

By the reckoning of some historians, Gen. George Washington never had more than thirty thousand troops under his command. About half that number—the size of an Army division today—was his typical strength.

British forces were not only better trained, but also usually larger. However, when British weaknesses were exposed, Washington struck. In 1781, with the aid of French warships blockading the Virginia coast, the Continental Army achieved a decisive victory over British forces at Yorktown.

Until the Constitution was adopted eight years later, the national government relied upon the states to provide ground troops. Creation of a permanent—or "standing"—Army was a subject of debate for decades.

A small force, the Army aided local militias against Indian tribes, watched a contested border with Canada, and led the exploration of the western reaches of the continent. It became more professional with the creation of the U.S. Military Academy at West Point in 1802.

Ten years later, the Napoleonic Wars in Europe spilled into the New World. During the War of 1812, U.S. forces struck north against Canada, while the British raided the Atlantic coast. British troops burned the nation's capital and bombarded Baltimore during a siege that led to the composition of "The Star-Spangled Banner."

Major campaigns were fought against the Seminole Indians in Florida during the early 1800s, while the Army formed cavalry units to deal with the Indians of the western plains.

An influx of U.S. settlers into what's now Texas—and then part of Mexico—triggered a war with Mexico in 1846. Army units went on the offensive in Mexican-controlled California and in Mexico proper, fighting all the way to Mexico City. Peace ended Mexico's claims to land north of the Rio Grande River.

At the eve of the Civil War, the army had about fifteen thousand people in uniform, the majority scattered in small units across the plains, with the rest along the Canadian border. More than a quarter of Army officers shifted their loyalties to the Confederacy when war broke out in 1861.

All the Confederacy had to do to win was to survive in the field. Beginning with the first battle of Bull Run in July 1861, Union forces took the battle to the enemy, from the shores of the Atlantic to the Mississippi and points farther west.

Shiloh, Vicksburg, and Chancellorsville were famous battlegrounds in the first half of the war. Gettysburg in Pennsylvania was the site of the Confederacy's great gamble to split the Union. The gamble failed, and the war continued two more years as Northern forces tightened the noose on the South. The end came with a formal surrender at Appomattox, Virginia, on April 9, 1865.

Following the war, the Army quickly dropped to a strength of about twenty-five thousand and stayed at that level for most of the quarter-century war with the American Indian that finally ended at Wounded Knee in December 1890.

Within less than a decade, the Army went from battling Indians to mounting operations against a major colonial power. Beginning in 1898, the Spanish-American War saw the U.S. Army deploy major units in Cuba and halfway around the world in the Philippine Islands. The Spanish-American War ended with the United States firmly established as a world power, thanks mostly to U.S. naval power.

At the start of World War I, the United States had less than a hundred thousand people in uniform (it would end the war with 3.7 million), no units as large as a division, and only nineteen officers in Army headquarters in Washington.

During thirteen months in combat in France, the U.S. Army, under the field command of Gen. John Pershing, functioned as a member of a coalition. The fabled American industry that would prove so decisive in World War II didn't exist then. Most of the nation's aircraft and artillery were of foreign manufacture.

Long before the Japanese attack at Pearl Harbor in December 1941, U.S. leaders were preparing for a war that had already spread over the Pacific rim and almost all of Europe. The first peacetime draft began in September 1940; American industry retooled to help the Allies.

The Army swelled to 11.2 million people and fought what amounted to two different wars during World War II—intense battles against Japanese infantrymen and larger, set-piece battles against more heavily equipped German and Italian forces.

The atomic bomb, whose development was supervised by the Army, changed forever the face of warfare—changed it, but didn't prevent it. Communist forces in North Korea tried to overwhelm a pro-Western government in the South in 1950. The United States was drawn into a bloody, three-year conflict, and several times it teetered on the brink of ruin. More than fifty thousand Americans died in a war that ended exactly where it started.

More wrenching was the Army's twenty-five-year involvement in South Vietnam, first as a supplier, then an advisor, finally as the dominant force in Southeast Asia. The U.S. Army never lost a major battle, but invading the aggressor was never an option.

Many of the lessons of the Vietnam War were played out, with greater success, in the 1991 Persian Gulf War. At a cost of less than 150 American lives, a American-led coalition defeated the fourth-largest army on the planet.

Today, the Army has about 480,000 people on active duty and deployed around the world to guard a peace that doesn't seem very peaceful.

(Source: *American Military History*, Army Historical Series [Washington, D.C.: Center for Military History, 1989.])

NAVY

On October 13, 1775 the Continental Congress adopted legislation for "a swift sailing vessel, to carry ten carriage guns . . . with eighty men." Thus began the U.S. Navy.

Even by that point in the Revolution, warships were setting sail to further the cause of the former colonists. Some ships were controlled by the new states, others by private citizens, a few by Army commanders.

By the end of the war, the Continental Navy had about forty vessels and claimed more than two hundred enemy ships captured. It was the French navy, however, that made the decisive contribution at sea, bottling up British forces from supply or evacuation.

Despite the new nation's reliance upon seagoing trade, Congress allowed the Navy to go out of business. The last warship was sold in 1785. Not until a quasi-war developed with the French over access to the Caribbean did the Navy come back into existence in 1797.

No sooner had the United States asserted its right to trade freely with the nations along its borders than its trading rights with more distant partners was challenged. For years, states in northern Africa had been raiding merchant ships and holding crews for ransom.

The struggle with those pirate-states along the Barbary Coast of Africa went on, sporadically, until 1815. Meanwhile, a greater threat had emerged. The British were also impeding trade and taking U.S. sailors from their ships. The border with British-controlled Canada was another site of friction between the two nations.

When those tensions erupted in the War of 1812, the fledgling navy faced a major test. Ships operating in the Great Lakes turned back a British invasion, while vessels along the Atlantic coast struggled against a blockade. The USS *Constitution* gained the nickname "Old Ironsides" during this war.

Throughout the first half of the 1800s, the Navy stopped ships bringing slaves from Africa. In the Caribbean, sailors fought a long-running conflict with pirates, who by one count had robbed more than three thousand vessels.

Another conflict almost forgotten today targeted the Seminole Indians in Florida and the Creek tribe in Alabama and Georgia. Small naval vessels, sometimes mere flat-bottomed barges and canoes, threaded their way through rivers and swamps with supplies and troops.

By the time the two-year war with Mexico began in 1846, the Navy was ready for more conventional combat. The fleet blockaded Mexican ports along the Gulf of Mexico and the Pacific Ocean. The Navy–Marine Corps team captured cities on the California coast, while at Vera Cruz over twelve thousand troops went ashore in a single-day amphibious landing.

The Civil War split the Navy, as people with Southern roots moved into the Confederate navy. Although school children learn the major land battles of the war, control of the seas—and the nation's major rivers—was a strategic objective for both sides. Five days after Confederate batteries fired on Fort Sumter, Pres. Abraham Lincoln ordered a blockade of the rebellious states.

The war featured the first use of a reconnaissance balloon tied to a naval vessel, the deployment of vessels carrying mortars to pound forts, improvements in steam-powered craft, and the first combat uses of the armor-plated warship, the submarine, and the torpedo.

As a handful of Confederate raiders played a deadly game of cat-and-mouse on the high seas, pitched battles were fought for control of major rivers, especially the Mississippi, between fleets of armored vessels and batteries ashore.

Barely four decades later, the Spanish-American War began with a naval incident—the mysterious destruction of the U.S. battleship *Maine* in Havana harbor in February 1898—and it would end with two decisive naval victories half a world apart. In May, a U.S. fleet destroyed the Spanish fleet in Manila Bay in the Philippines. Two months later, another U.S. fleet annihilated the Spanish naval force in the Caribbean with a series of battles near Santiago, Cuba.

The aftermath of that victory was costly. The United States occupied the Philippines after the war and immediately fell into a three-year guerrilla war against Filipinos eager for independence. This country's new-won prominence as an international naval power also drew it into combat in mainland China in 1900 to help relieve the besieged representatives in from Beijing of a loose confederation of European powers. U.S. vessels regularly patrolled Chinese rivers for more than fifty years to protect U.S. interests.

Like the Spanish-American War, World War II began for the United States with a naval disaster—the surprise Japanese attack against Pearl Harbor—and ended only after major naval victories turned the tide of war. U.S. and Japanese fleets fought major battles across the Pacific. In the Atlantic, the threat came from German submarines. The navy maintained a lifeline of convoys that supported the Allies in the early days of the war, then relied upon a preponderance of naval power to enable amphibious landings in North Africa, Sicily, Italy and eventually, the Normandy coast of France.

The Korean War, which began in June 1950, saw U.S. vessels form a blockade around the entire peninsula and support U.S. ground forces with carrier-based aircraft. Naval expertise made possible a dramatic, behind-the-lines amphibious landing at Inchon and, later, the evacuation of nearly two hundred thousand people at Hungnam.

In 1962, Pres. John Kennedy called upon the Navy to blockade Cuba to force the Soviet Union to remove nuclear missiles from the island. Without firing a shot, the Navy made one of its greatest contributions in the second half of the twentieth century.

The naval lessons of Korea were reapplied in the Vietnam War, with the added ingredient of a large force of small vessels on the rivers.

The end of that war saw smaller, shorter engagements in Grenada, Panama, Somalia, and Haiti, followed by the 1991 Gulf War, which once again relied upon the Navy to blockade the enemy and called upon its full resources—from carrier-based planes and submarine-launched cruise missiles to the big guns of a few battleships—to pummel the enemy.

At the start of the new millennium, the Navy had about 380,000 men and women on active duty.

(Source: Stephen Howarth, *To Shining Sea* [Norman: University of Oklahoma Press, 1991].)

AIR FORCE

The Air Force celebrates its official birthday on September 18. That was the day in 1947 that it became an independent member of the military, equal to the Army and Navy. For nearly a century before that moment, it had existed in various ways as a portion of the Army.

In 1861, men rose above the battlefields of the Civil War in balloons filled with hot air to observe enemy positions and the movements of troops. Soon, they began directing artillery fire.

Called the Balloon Service, the nation's first organized fliers stayed on the job after the war. Soldiers in observation balloons played a role in Teddy Roosevelt's famous battle of San Juan Hill, in Cuba, during the Spanish-American War.

In 1909, six years after the Wright Brothers flew the first airplane at Kitty Hawk, North Carolina, the Army gave the brothers thirty thousand dollars for the first military airplane. Heavier-than-air craft entered the military's inventory.

The new airplane chased the Mexican bandit Pancho Villa along the Texas-Mexico border, with little success. It was in Europe, where nations were inching toward war during the early days of the last century, that the fledgling airplane proved itself as a military weapon.

When World War I began, the United States had barely two hundred airplanes, all inferior to the machines flown by European forces. Americans were joining the English and French militaries to fly. A famous group of U.S. fliers made up the Lafayette Escadrille in the French air force.

On some missions, half the pilots were killed or wounded. Deaths from mechanical failures were more common than combat losses. Still, the

United States ended the war having built nearly twelve thousand airplanes. Seventy-one Americans shot down at least five enemy aircraft and achieved the coveted title of "ace."

Like the rest of the U.S. military, the aerial services, then part of the Army, were cut back after the war, but the U.S. commitment to developing this new weapon continued.

Brig. Gen. Billy Mitchell, who had commanded a large portion of U.S. air forces in Europe during the war, proved the power of the airplane in 1921 in several highly publicized flights that sank captured German battleships. General Mitchell wasn't very kind in his opinions of people who disagreed with him, and that led to his equally publicized court-martial.

The airplane was a mature, deadly weapon when the Japanese bombing of Pearl Harbor on December 7, 1941, brought the United States into World War II. Most of the U.S. airplanes in the Pacific were destroyed in Japanese attacks during the first days of the war. In Europe, American pilots were again serving in the air forces of allies before our country entered the war.

By August 1942, the first summer of the war, U.S. bombers stationed in England were bombing targets across Europe. Some of the attacks of the U.S. Eighth Air Force became legendary. In one mission against industrial targets in Schweinfurt, Germany, more than a quarter of the planes were lost. By the time U.S. troops landed at Normandy on June 6, 1944, bombing had eliminated much of the famed Luftwaffe, or German air force.

In the war against Japan, cargo planes were airlifting supplies to allies in China by flying from India over the Himalaya Mountains; pilots called that flying "the Hump." Gen. Douglas MacArthur, who commanded about half of the U.S. forces in the Pacific, decided which island to invade next by the range of airplanes operating from the last island captured.

Retaliation for the attack against Pearl Harbor began five months after the start of the war, when sixteen specially equipped bombers under the command of Lt. Col. Jimmy Doolittle took off from an aircraft carrier that didn't normally carry those long-range bombers.

Doolittle's famous raid on Tokyo was more important for U.S. morale than for damaging targets. Eventually, however, U.S. forces launched punishing attacks against the Japanese homeland that reached a highpoint with a series of raids against Japanese cities. A single attack against Tokyo in March 1945 killed nearly a hundred thousand.

Rather than risk U.S. troops in a deadly landing on the beaches of Japan, Pres. Harry Truman authorized the first use of the atomic bomb. A bomber called *Enola Gay* (the name was that of the pilot's mother) dropped an atomic bomb on Hiroshima on August 6, 1945. But Japan didn't surrender.

Three days later, another bomber carried a second atomic weapon to Nagasaki, and the war ended.

More than two million tons of bombs were dropped by U.S. aircraft during the war. A little more than two years after the end of World War II, on September 18, 1947, the Air Force became a separate branch of the military.

Concern with attacking an enemy's homeland during a war—called "strategic bombing"—continued to be a major interest of the Air Force in the postwar era, although the bombs were nuclear, and they were joined with nuclear-tipped missiles.

But not all problems can be solved with bombs. In June 1948, the Soviet Union blocked all ground transportation to the city of Berlin, and the 2.5 million inhabitants faced either starvation or war. Instead, President Truman ordered a mercy mission that became known as the "Berlin Airlift." In eleven months, Air Force cargo planes carried more than two million tons of food and supplies to the city.

Different tests came in 1950 with the Korean War, in 1964 with the Vietnam War, and 1991 with the Gulf War. Each conflict created its own challenges and Air Force heroes who overcame them.

As the nation moves into a new century, the Air Force has about 370,000 people on active duty, all dedicated, like those first pioneers who rose above the battlefields of the Civil War in hot-air balloons, to use the skies to prevail in conflicts.

(Source: Stephen L. McFarland, *A Concise History of the U.S. Air Force* [Air Force History and Museums Program, 1997.])

MARINE CORPS

The U.S. Marine Corps celebrates its birthday on November 10. On that day in 1775, the Continental Congress authorized the new government to get "two battalions of Marines . . . able to serve to advantage at sea."

By that time, European nations had had seagoing infantrymen on their combat vessels, off and on, for several hundred years. The British had created their first Marine outfit nearly a hundred and fifty years before.

Marines were sharpshooters who climbed into the rigging of sailing ships and picked off the crew of enemy vessels, especially officers. They led boarding parties and served as replacements on gun crews. Sometimes they fought on land. On board their own ships, they were the policemen who kept the crew in line.

Barely six months after their creation, Marines made their first amphibious landing, in the Bahamas. Units fought alongside George Washington's

Continental Army, but mostly the Marines were recruited and controlled by each ship's captain.

Like the Navy, the Marine Corps went out of existence for a few years after America won its independence, but the new nation was unable to stay out of conflict.

Soon, the Marine Corps was reestablished, and Marines were fighting pirates off northern Africa (enshrined in their hymn as "the shores of Tripoli") and French warships on the Atlantic.

During the War of 1812, Marines served on warships that asserted U.S. control over the Great Lakes. When the new nation's capital was threatened by the British army, contingents of Marines fought alongside the U.S. Army in an unsuccessful effort to stop the invaders. More successful were the Marines who joined Andrew Jackson's defense of New Orleans in the last U.S. victory of that war.

The period between the War of 1812 and the Civil War was a busy time for this new branch of the U.S. military. Ashore and afloat, Marines fought a seven-year war against the Seminole Indians of Florida, who were resisting efforts to remove them from their land. They helped enforce U.S. efforts to stop slave traders. From Africa, to the Caribbean and the South Atlantic, Marines went ashore to protect U.S. citizens.

When fighting began with Mexico in 1846, Marines perfected their tactics in seizing port defenses, often with makeshift units drawn from several vessels. As the war intensified, Marines fought alongside Army infantry units closing in on Mexico City (remembered as "the halls of Montezuma" in the Marine hymn).

Like the rest of the nation, the Marine Corps was fragmented by the Civil War. The Confederacy had its own Marine Corps, built around veterans of the federal force. The Union's Marines fought as infantry at Bull Run, but mostly they kept to their traditional jobs aboard ship, including those engaged in pitched battles for control of the Mississippi River.

In the aftermath of the Civil War, as the Navy transitioned from sailing ships to iron-hulled vessels, the Marines' role as individual sharpshooters positioned in a ship's rigging was eliminated. In its place, the nation was calling upon Marines to protect the nation's interest in far-flung foreign lands.

Composer John Philip Sousa became leader of the Marine Band in 1880. Two years later, the Naval Academy began to commission new graduates into the Marines.

By 1898, the nation was at war again, this time with Spain. A key landing at Guantanamo Bay in Cuba solidified in the minds of strategic thinkers the value of amphibious assaults. Victory over Spain meant the acquisition of the Philippine Islands, and Marines fought heated battles there against guerrillas striving for independence.

China and Mexico were the scenes of major deployments of Marines under fire, and there were lesser actions throughout the Caribbean.

World War I lasted six months for the Marines. But it was long enough to suffer ten thousand casualties and stories that slipped into legend about places like Belleau Woods and St. Mihiel, and the "devil dogs" of the Fourth Brigade.

More legendary fights came during World War II—Guadalcanal, Tarawa, Iwo Jima, Okinawa—as the Marines handled much of the ground combat in the Pacific theater. Nearly twenty thousand Marines were killed during the war, almost as many Marines as died in all the other wars of the twentieth century combined. Eighty-two men earned the Medal of Honor.

The Korean War saw Marines in combat on the Asian mainland and the entry of another legend—"Chosin Reservoir"—into the lore of the Corps to commemorate the fighting withdrawal of forces during a winter of indescribable harshness.

During the Vietnam War, once again Marines moved next to Army forces in the field and shouldered the role of regular infantrymen. At the hill known as Khe Sahn, about six thousand Marines tied down tens of thousands of North Vietnamese regular soldiers who sought to overrun the Marines' position. The two-month siege yielded 205 dead defenders and nearly ten thousand North Vietnamese fatalities.

In the postwar era, Marines assumed for the first time a formal role in NATO's plans for the defense of Europe. Marines took responsibility for aiding the Scandinavian countries if fighting broke out.

Meanwhile, there were plenty of hot spots into which Marines were sent to cool things down: Lebanon in 1982, Grenada in 1983, Panama in 1989, and finally the Middle East after Iraq invaded Kuwait in 1990.

More than ninety thousand Marines were deployed to the region for the Gulf War. Amphibious units aboard ship kept the Iraqis guessing about U.S. plans. When the Army's mechanized forces swung wide across the desert at the start of the ground war, the Marines punched through the heart of Iraq's fortifications around Kuwait.

In the aftermath of the Gulf War, Marines stayed busy with large humanitarian missions and smaller combat-type deployments. They led the way in 1994 when U.S. forces landed in Haiti to restore democracy, and Marine aviators were part of the forces that bombed Kosovo during 1999.

"Semper Fidelis"—"Always Faithful"—is the Marine Corps motto. Fidelity and heroism have been interwoven for more than two centuries in the record of the Marine Corps's service to the nation. About 170,000 Marines serve on active duty today.

(Sources: Allan R. Millett, *Semper Fidelis* (New York: Free Press, 1980); *Brief History of the United States Marine Corps* [Washington, D.C.: History and Museum Division, USMC, nd.])

COAST GUARD

At least five different organizations performed work we now associate with the U.S. Coast Guard in the 125 years before the service's formal creation on January 28, 1915. The Revenue Cutter Service, the Lighthouse Service, the Steamboat Inspection Service, the Bureau of Navigation, and the Lifesaving Service—these are groups that shaped the modern Coast Guard.

One of the first acts of Congress after adopting the Constitution in 1789 was to put all lighthouses under federal control. Barely a year later, lawmakers authorized "a system of cutters" to make sure the federal government received taxes (called "tariffs") on goods brought into the service.

These "cutters" became the Revenue Service. Interestingly, from 1790 to 1798 they were the only naval force the new nation had. The U.S. Navy had been disbanded in 1785 after the end of the Revolutionary War and wouldn't reappear until 1798.

The cutters were involved in eliminating the pirates who still operated along the Atlantic coast. Cutters attacked the home bases of some of them in the Caribbean. After 1807, the vessels were also used to prevent the shipment of slaves to the United States.

During the War of 1812, cutters fought British warships at sea. During wars against the Seminole Indians in Florida (1836–1842) and with Mexico (1846–1848), cutters ferried troops to shore in combat, a role they would resume in a major way during World War II.

Although "environmental protection" is a phrase that came into common use only in the post-Vietnam era, the forbearers of the Coast Guard were doing that nearly two centuries ago. In the 1820s, they were charged with stopping people who tried to strip public lands of their timber. When the United States bought Alaska from the Russians, the Revenue Service enforced game laws and, eventually, fishing regulations.

In 1831, the Revenue Service was formally directed to cruise the coastal waters in search of vessels in distress, although it had been doing that since its earliest cruises.

Also accelerating during the country's first half-century was the work of the Lifesaving Service, which was another ancestor of the Coast Guard. In those days, navigational maps were unreliable. The most dangerous parts of any cruise were when a ship was closest to shore. Hundreds of lives were lost every year when ships were driven ashore during storms and pounded apart on rocks and beaches. Some of the most awesome stories of bravery at sea involve men who rowed lifesaving boats into the churning waters of a hurricane to rescue the passengers and crews of disabled ships.

Another milestone in Coast Guard history, which came before the Civil War, was the inspection of commercial vessels. Early steamboats were deadly; their boilers were prone to explode. One 1865 disaster on the Mississippi claimed nearly 1,500 lives, almost as many as the sinking of the passenger liner *Titanic* forty-seven years later.

Like the other military services, the crews of the cutters were torn when the Civil War divided the loyalties of Americans. The vessels continued flying the Union flag. But the Confederacy created its own fleet of cutters, which spent much of their time raiding other ships instead of collecting taxes.

When the Spanish-American War was fought in 1898, cutters sailed with U.S. fleets that attacked Spanish ports in Cuba and the Philippines.

Less than two decades later, after the United States entered World War I, vessels of the fledgling Coast Guard were dispatched to the British colony of Gibraltar, at the mouth of the Mediterranean Sea, to escort convoys from there to the British Isles and back again.

One of the worst naval disasters of the World War I befell the cutter *Tampa*, which was sunk by the torpedoes of a German submarine with the loss of all 115 crewmen.

America went "dry" during the period between world wars, when the Twenty-third Amendment made alcohol illegal in the United States. Coast Guard cutters were charged with stopping "rum runners," in deadly chases on the high seas reminiscent of antidrug patrols in our time.

World War II again brought the Coast Guard under navy control with a massive expansion. More than eight hundred Coast Guard cutters served during the war, and Coast Guardsmen manned more than six hundred other vessels. They were credited with sinking twelve German submarines while patrolling the Atlantic seaboard.

Coast Guardsmen were at the controls of landing craft in all the major amphibious landings of the War, from North Africa, Italy, and France to the deadly assaults in the Pacific. On D-Day off the Normandy beaches, Coast Guard cutters rescued more than 1,500 troops from damaged landing craft.

The service's role during the Korean War was limited to helping create the South Korean Coast Guard and manning search-and-rescue stations on the Pacific routes used by the maritime industry and the airlines to send troops and equipment to the war zone.

Slightly more than a decade later, the war in Vietnam brought a greater commitment from the Coast Guard. Its shallow-draft boats were ideal for operating in the rivers that crisscrossed Southeast Asia. Coast Guard vessels ferried troops, inspected junks for weapons, and helped forces ashore with their firepower. With nearly all of the goods and equipment supporting U.S. forces arriving by sea, Vietnam soon had some of the busiest ports in the world, and Coast Guard personnel guaranteed the storage of dangerous cargo and warded off enemy divers.

Some of the Coast Guard's contributions during the Vietnam War were based upon its peacetime missions. The U.S. Coast Guard set up buoys and other aids to navigation in the waters of Southeast Asia while creating a network of transmitters used in long-range navigation.

While continuing its traditional missions after the war, the Coast Guard shifted its focus to the Caribbean. Cutters intercepted drugs and refugees heading to the shores of the United States.

When Kuwait was invaded in 1990 to begin the Gulf War, Coast Guard cutters took part in the international blockade that cut off Iraq from seaborne supplies. When Iraq deliberately flooded the Persian Gulf with oil, Coast Guardsmen took the lead in trying to prevent an ecological catastrophe.

With thirty-eight thousand men and women on active duty today, the Coast Guard has reverted to its busy peacetime missions. *"Semper Paratus"*—Always Prepared—is the service's motto. It could be "Always Needed."

(Sources: Robert E. Johnson, *Guardians of the Sea* [Annapolis, Md.: Naval Institute Press, 1987].)

★ ★ Appendix E ★ ★

MILITARY LIFE IN
THE MOVIES

For good and ill, we often see our society through a celluloid filter. The products of Hollywood do more than amuse and fill time. They can help us make sense of the world around us, sometimes in subtle ways, other times with all the bombast of a big-screen extravaganza.

Here are some examples of the way the military has fared in major motion pictures. This selection was made of movies that tried to show various aspects of military life. Not included in this selection are war movies. Combat is an exception in the career of anyone in uniform.

ACADEMIES

Dress Gray. One-star generals do not stand at attention to talk on the telephone to two-star generals. That's the least of the factual misstatements in this made-for-television movie about sexual assault, murder, and cover-ups at a fictional academy that's a thinly veiled model of the U.S. Military Academy at West Point. It's all Hollywood, and nothing military.

Francis Goes to West Point. For reasons lost to memory, there once was a series of movies about a talking mule. He was no loveable four-footed fellow but a cranky cuss who showed how jackasses got their reputation. The scene in which Francis the mule puts cadet Donald O'Connor through the basic rifle commands is still fun.

The Long Gray Line. Hollywood took a sentimental look at West Point in this story of an enlisted man who was assigned there for fifty years. Although the movie was made in the 1950s, much of the footage of cadet life could have been shot fifty days ago. It's corny in places, but a must-see for any would-be plebes or midshipmen.

The Lords of Discipline. Hazing of new cadets has always been rough. At one academy, they can teach terrorist organizations a thing or two. But the relationships between cadets are usually realistic, with the older ones looking out for the younger ones, under the watchful eyes of the instructors.

Major Payne. Damon Wayans is a "trained weapon of destruction" downsized into running the Junior ROTC program at Madison Preparatory School. Lacking in social skills and not too bright, Maj. Benson Payne turns a handful of teenaged misfits into a crack drill team, finds love, and decides civilian life isn't too bad. A predictable plot woven into a gentle look at some clichés about the military.

The Private War of Major Benson. Sheraton Military Academy gets Charlton Heston as a hard-drinking, hard-nosed, hard-to-live-with combat veteran sent to run its ROTC program. Comparing this mid-1950s movie with the modern *Major Payne* says little about the military but a lot about Hollywood.

Taps. When Bunker Hill Military Academy is slated to be closed, the cadets break into the weapons room and try to save the school by having it destroyed. Still, it's a good look at the interplay between students at these high school-level academies. It has early roles for Timothy Hutton, Tom Cruise, and Sean Penn. Interestingly, Penn is the stable one, and Cruise is the nut case.

BOOT CAMP

Biloxi Blues. Playwright Neil Simon spins a realistic tale of boot camp that focuses on the relationship between trainees. The setting is the end of World War II, the one-liners are snappy, and the insights are still relevant. There are strong performances by Matthew Broderick as a recruit and Christopher Walken as an offbeat, war-weary drill sergeant.

The DI. Jack Webb is Tech. Sgt. Jim Moore, a drill sergeant with a heart of gold in the late 1950s who struggles to keep a malcontent with potential in uniform. A dated view of boot camp that's now of interest for one reason: Webb's depiction of a Marine drill instructor was for decades the standard by which drill sergeants everywhere secretly judged themselves.

Forrest Gump. Tom Hanks is Forrest Gump, the man whose life's story goes from the founding of the Ku Klux Klan to the invention of the happy-face. Gump fits into boot camp "like one of these round pegs," poking fun at everything in olive drab. Gary Sineses's unflinching portrayal of a paralyzed soldier makes this movie special to many veterans.

Full Metal Jacket (Pt. 1). Lee Ermy, a retired Marine Corps drill instructor, was hired as a consultant by filmmaker Stanley Kubrick to add realism to this movie's depiction of boot camp. Kubrick ended up giving the DI's role to Ermy, who incorporated many of his training one-liners into the script. Don't take the physical abuse literally—that's Hollywood, not boot camp.

Private Benjamin. Goldie Hawn is Pvt. Judie Benjamin, a daughter of privilege who grows up fast in the U.S. Army. More a coming-of-age movie than a military movie, all of its beginning and most of its ending has nothing to do with the armed forces. But Hawn's one-liners about boot camp are priceless.

Renaissance Man. Danny DeVito is a civilian teacher under contract to the Army to keep some marginal recruits in boot camp by teaching them Shakespeare. No, it's not very plausible, but at least it's consistent: it's not funny, either.

Stripes. Bill Murray is John Winger, a smart-talking huckster who joins the Army and becomes a hero, although he stays a smart-talking huckster. The movie's depiction of boot camp is actually more realistic than many films for Rambo wanna-bes. The scene in which Murray's character leads his unit at the graduation-day parade at boot camp makes this video well worth the rental fee.

To the Shores of Tripoli. During World War II, Hollywood tried to make Marine Corps boot camp more appealing in this silly film, which shows recruits sneaking away from their training for a night on the town in tuxedos. See this only if you have a relative who talks about how tough it was in the old days.

OTHER TRAINING

G.I. Jane. Demi Moore is Lt. Jordan O'Neil, the fictional first woman to join the Navy's elite SEAL commandos. The military refused to help the movie's producers, because the way trainees were mistreated in the film was unrealistic even by Hollywood's standards. Still, the movie is a favorite among women in the military for its sympathetic portrayal of their problems.

No Time for Sergeants. Before there was Forrest Gump, even before there was Gomer Pyle, there was Will Stockdale, played by a young Andy Griffith as a hillbilly-turned-airman. The story is set mostly in a 1950's Classification Center, a predecessor of today's MEPS Centers. The stage version of this movie is still making the rounds of the community theaters. Watch for the short appearance by Griffith's future *Mayberry* co-star, Don Knotts.

An Officer and a Gentleman. No bad guys, just a lot of people growing up, that's one feature of this Richard Gere movie about Officer Candidate School for naval aviators. It's an adult depiction of the teamwork expected in the military. Louis Gossett, Jr., won an Academy Award for his on-the-money portrayal of a Marine drill instructor.

Strategic Air Command. War is a fluke, but training is a constant for the military. This Jimmy Stewart movie from the mid-1950s captures the intensity of the peacetime training tempo. It's a little dated around the edges, but footage of B-36s and B-47s make this a must-see for flying buffs. A from-the-cockpit scene of flying in a storm is still a solid pilot's-eye view of flying.

Top Gun. Not since the "rally round the boys" movies of World War II has Hollywood made a major film that puts military folks in such a positive light. This Tom Cruise film captures the testosterone-saturated air of a flight unit in training. It also shows the brains needed to wear a fighter pilot's helmet. Scenes of actual operations aboard an aircraft carrier were filmed with a poet's eye.

MILITARY LIFE

Cadence. Charlie Sheen is a young soldier figuring out his place in the world, but he spends most of this movie in a military stockade in Germany. There are good touches in places, but the movie gets strange at the end when the tough sergeant, played by Sheen's real-life dad, Martin Sheen, turns psychopathic.

The Caine Mutiny. Only one scene from this mid-1950s classic involves combat, so we've included it on our list. It's Hollywood's most powerful look at the meaning of loyalty to a commander. Check it out at the video rental store. If your attitude toward Humphrey Bogart's character, Captain Queeg, doesn't change in the last fifteen minutes, you weren't paying attention.

Chasers. In the maritime services, a "chaser" is someone transporting a prisoner to jail or a court-martial. *Baywatch* beauty Erika Eleniak is the prisoner in this tale, which makes "chaser" the proper word for her guards. In the real Navy, her guards would have their own legal problems from calling female coworkers "sexy" and "gorgeous."

A Few Good Men. Loyalty to the unit and the limits of orders are at the heart of this courtroom drama that begins with the murder of a Marine by squad members: serious issues and Demi Moore, all in one movie. Jack Nicholson's portrayal of the tightly wound colonel is a classic, but future recruits should know that any real-life versions of Nicholson's character were ordered a long time ago into psychiatric treatment.

Francis in the Navy. If you can believe that a mule can wander around a naval base unobserved, then you won't have trouble believing the mule also talks. It's watchable now mostly for the supporting role played by a boyish Clint Eastwood.

From Here to Eternity. Were "the good old days" really that good? Take a look at the living conditions for these Hawaii-based soldiers in the weeks before the start of World War II. You can understand why your grandfather thinks today's military is soft.

Gardens of Stone. The title comes from a grim nickname for Arlington National Cemetery. The movie takes place during the turbulent middle of the Vietnam War. A standout for the honest depiction of garrison life and the interplay among professionals, it also includes insights about—and real footage of—the Army's famed "Old Guard," which guards the Tomb of the Unknowns at Arlington.

The Great Santini. In the thousands of novels and hundreds of movies about the military, few writers have noticed that most soldiers have children. This is an adaptation of writer Pat Conroy's sometimes painful novel about growing up in a military family. This is mandatory viewing for anyone who thinks that a touch of boot camp will improve home life.

Heartbreak Ridge. Clint Eastwood directed and starred as Gunnery Sgt. Tom Hightower. Set in the Marine Corps immediately before the Grenada invasion, its view of the peacetime military is amazingly wrong. Future recruits beware: privates don't physically threaten their sergeants, units don't mutiny in garrison, and nobody, but nobody, fails to notice a Medal of Honor on a uniform.

Hot Shots. They wear uniforms, salute each other, and fly fighter jets. Those are about the only connections between the characters in this comedy and the real-world military. It's a funny movie, but *Private Benjamin* is funnier and tells you more about military life.

In the Army Now. Pauly Shore does to the Army . . . what Pauly Shore usually does to the rest of the world. It's surprisingly accurate in catching the tone of life among troops, and by Hollywood standards not too bad a depiction of boot camp and Army life.

The Last Detail. Look on this Jack Nicholson movie as an earlier, grittier version of *Chasers.* More a 1970s parable of life as trip to a prison than a military movie, it gives some interesting glimpses of an earlier life in uniform. It's also funnier than *Chasers.*

Mister Roberts. As a Navy cargo ship sails the rear areas of the Pacific during World War II, Henry Fonda is a likable second in command shielding his crew from an erratic captain. But compare Fonda's role to Van Johnson's second in command in *The Caine Mutiny.* Might he really be a bad officer who encourages the crew to disrespect their captain?

Sgt. Bilko. The deal-up-his-sleeve NCO was a cliche for the World War II generation. From that background came one of the most popular television series of the 1950s about Sgt. Ernie Bilko and the pandemonium he brought to a motor pool. Steve Martin reprised Phil Silver's original TV role with the same good-hearted avarice. A fun movie.

A Soldier's Story. The scene is an Army post in Louisiana during the height of World War II. The characters are "tan Yanks," as some called African-American soldiers. It's an uncomfortable look at a society in transition. Veteran actor Adolph Caesar's portrayal of an insecure tyrant makes this worth the price of a video rental.

The Teahouse of the August Moon. Living in another country is a big attraction of military service. In this film from the mid-1950s, which has a stage version still touring the nation's community theaters, an Army civil affairs unit tries to modernize an Okinawa village after World War II. The movie is perhaps most interesting for the Okinawa villager played by a young, smiling, slim Marlon Brando.

This Is the Army. This Ronald Reagan movie (he plays a soldier, not a politician) is based upon the "Soldier Shows" that were a staple of an earlier era, when the only way for troops to get entertainment was to create it themselves. Great songs by Irving Berlin, but there are a few painful moments with heavyweight great Joe Louis and troops in "blackface" in a minstrel show.

COMING HOME

Article 99. Think of the television series *M*A*S*H,* set in the states in a VA hospital—without any laughs. The creators of this made-for-TV movie should have played it for yucks. Imagine doctors breaking into a lab in their own hospital because people are dying for lack of pacemakers that are being given to monkeys in a research program—that's the stuff of dark comedy, not docudramas.

Best Days of Our Lives. Have you thought the GIs of World War II came home to marching bands and GI Bill-financed homes in the suburbs? Not so. By the standards of the postwar era, Hollywood cast a gritty eye on the problems of returning servicemen in this classic film. Double-amputee Harold Russell won an Academy Award for his role as a disabled sailor.

Born on the 4th of July. Tom Cruise plays a real-life paralyzed Vietnam veteran in this bundle of antiwar cliches. The scene in which Cruise's character argues with another vet over who killed the most babies would be funny if it weren't so sincere. *Francis Goes to West Point* is a braver, more realistic look at the military.

Coming Home. If you want to understand what the Vietnam protests of the 1960s were like, rent this classic antiwar movie. Everyone supporting the military is immoral and stupid. Everyone opposed to it is noble, with-it, and fun. This Oscar-winner had nothing truthful to say about the Vietnam-era military; it is even less relevant today.

First Blood. A veteran is treated poorly in Hope, Oregon, during the height of the Vietnam War. By the end of the movie, the town burns to the ground, and the vet, a recently discharged fellow named John Rambo (yes, that Rambo) is battered, bloodied, but unbowed. Here's the least successful transition to the private sector on record.

Green Eyes. A tragic aftermath of every war are the children fathered by U.S. servicemen overseas. This neglected little tale is about a crippled veteran who returns to Vietnam after the war to find his half-Vietnamese son. The few flashbacks to combat conform to Hollywood's view of Vietnam vets as war criminals, but the rest of the film can be touching.

The War at Home. Add this to the list of Vietnam movies by people who thought you had to be antimilitary in order to be antiwar. Worse, it's a laundry list of things not to do or say to a psychologically troubled veteran. The words "professional help" weren't part of the script.

OKAY, SOME WAR MOVIES

Based solely on the criteria of helping people understand what combat is really like, this is the author's selection of most honest movies:

- *Saving Private Ryan*. Everyone's favorite about World War II's D-Day invasion at Normandy.
- *Gettysburg*. A made-for-TV movie that puts the viewer in the ranks for the Civil War's decisive battle.
- *The Last Mohican*. Ever wonder what it was like in the early days of this country? This movie shows it.
- *Das boot*. About a German submarine crew during World War II. A powerful tale, it will change your idea of submarine service.

★ ★ Appendix F ★ ★

MILITARY JOBS AND CIVILIAN JOBS

Army

Duties	Qualifications	Civilian Jobs
Air Defense Artillery		
Operates and maintains electrical equipment. Communicates with air-traffic controllers. Monitors computers and telemetry.	Proficient in mathematics. Comfortable with electronics and mechanical devices. Stable. Good observation and reasoning skills.	Radar operator, data processing repair, maintenance of electrical equipment, repair radios, radar, telemetry equipment.
Ammunition Handler		
Stores and maintains explosive materials. Some oversight of shipping and distribution, plus supporting documentation.	Mechanical aptitude. Knowledge of computers helpful. Good vision, dexterity and emotional stability.	Construction work, demolition, storage of toxic materials. Inspection. Any work requiring attention to detail.
Armor		
Operates and maintains heavy equipment. Interprets maps. Member of reconnaissance team and security force.	Good physical fitness. Mechanical skill, good with mathematics and communications. Good working with a team.	Operate or repair of heavy equipment. Truck mechanic. Some electrical, optical work. Security. Supervise related fields.
Combat Engineering		
Constructs, repairs and maintains roads, bridges, port facilities, pipelines, supply tanks. Some demolition.	Solid mathematical skills. Good with carpentry, mechanical challenges. Some drawing and drafting helpful.	Construction worker, heavy equipment operator, drafter, rigger, bridge repair, highway repair, lumber worker, blaster.
Communications / Electronic Warfare		
Installs, operates and maintains computers, electronics, radios, testing, measuring and calibration equipment.	Aptitude for radio and television repair. Understanding of electronics and blueprints. Eligible for highest security clearances.	Radio control room technician, radio mechanic, transmitter repair. Repair and inspect other electrical equipment.
Field Artillery		
Operates and maintains radar and meteorological equipment. Operates unique computer programs and radios.	Mathematical skills essential. Mechanical aptitude helpful. Meteorological, computer and communications skills necessary.	Surveyor, topographic drafter, cartographer, meteorologist, radio operation. General computer or radio fields.
Infantry		
Works in closely coordinated teams, requiring adaptability, stability, good verbal communications, understanding of people.	Highest state of physical fitness. Mechanical aptitude helpful. Knows how to work with people. Communicates well, handles stress.	Police, fire or security work. Dispatcher. Fitness instructor, counselor or human relations specialist. Any team-based effort.
Intelligence		
Gathers and interprets information. Some interpretation of imagery and working with POWs. Stores, displays information.	Ability to communicate clearly in word and writing. Comfortable with ambiguity. Can be cleared for highest security access.	Investigator, journalist, researcher. Any job with premium on stability. Civilian law enforcement or intelligence agencies.

Sources: *Profile: Life in the Armed Forces*, DoD High School News Service, Norfolk, Va., and *Military Careers*, Defense Department, Washington, D.C. (1998 edition).

Navy

Duties	Qualifications	Civilian Jobs
Boatswain's Mate		
Performs basic seamanship tasks. Operates small boats, stores cargo, handles ropes. Variety of jobs aboard larger vessels.	Good physical fitness. Basic understanding of algebra and mathematics helpful. Works as part of team. Comfortable with heights.	Similar jobs with shipping companies, Merchant Marine, cruise lines. Stevedore, cargo handler, winch operator.
Gunner's Mate		
Operates and maintains missile launchers, cannon. Some work with hydraulics direction-finding gear and electrical systems.	Mechanical aptitude a must. Understanding of mathematics, electronics and optical systems good. Strong attention to detail.	Storage, maintenance of weapons and explosives. Any electrical or mechanical work. Civilian contractors. Police, fire departments.
Hull Maintenance		
Makes and installs shipboard structures, plumbing and related systems. Tests metallic materials. Inspects and stores material.	High mechanical aptitude. General knowledge of sheet metal, carpentry, plumbing. Geometry, mathematics and chemistry helpful.	Plumbing and construction work. Nuclear reactor technician. Welder. Technician in public utilities. Cruise ships.
Intelligence		
Gathers and interprets information. Prepares maps and graphics. Analyzes and displays imagery. Writes intelligence reports.	Ability to communicate clearly in word and writing. Comfortable with ambiguity. Can be cleared for highest security access.	Investigator, journalist, researcher. Any job with premium on stability. Civilian law enforcement or intelligence agencies.
Operations Specialist		
Operates surveillance equipment, aids to navigation. Coordinates aircraft operations. Maintains status boards.	Prolonged attention to detail. Knowledge of physics, mathematics, radio and electronics helpful. Some radio repair.	Radio operator. Aircraft controller. Statistical display and archiving of information. Some repair and maintenance.
Quartermaster		
Steers ship. Navigator. Oversees lookouts. Stands watch in bridge. Uses radio and navigational aids. Some maintenance.	Good vision and hearing. Ability to communicate clearly. Strong "people" skills, and understanding of electronics, mathematics.	Operation of any maritime vessel, from barge to cruise ship. Any job relying on judgment and ability to make snap decisions.
Sonar Technician		
Operates and maintains underwater detection equipment. Interprets and stores information. Some maintenance.	Excellent hearing and ability to communicate well. Aptitude with electronics and mechanical devices. Shopwork.	Radio operator, oil-well operations. User of advanced electronics and computer system. Some maintenance jobs.
Storekeeper		
Maintains supply operation, from ordering and receiving to inventories and quality control. Uses computers and mechanical equipment.	Comfortable with computers. Able to type. Basic bookkeeping. General business studies and math. Ability to write clearly.	Any shipping or inventory operation. Invoice, purchasing agent, bookkeeper or stock control clerk.

Sources: Profile: Life in the Armed Forces, DoD High School News Service, Norfolk, Va., and *Military Careers*, Defense Department, Washington, D.C. (1998 edition).

Air Force

Duties	Qualifications	Civilian Jobs
Aircrew		
Frequent flight in refueling, gun control, loadmaster, para-rescue. In-flight repair of mechanical equipment and electronics.	Good physical condition. Comfortable in tight spaces. Aptitude for mechanics, electrical systems, computers, radio operations.	Depends upon specific military duties and training. Broad range of jobs in mechanical repair, electronics, computers.
Aircrew Protection Specialist		
Maintenance of ejection and life-support equipment, survival gear. Instruction, some maintenance of electronics.	Strong mechanical, electrical and computer skills. Some woodsmanship. Comfortable with explosives.	No direct civilian equivalent. Police, fire department, construction work. Any job relying upon computers, mechanics, electronics.
Avionics Technician		
Installs, maintains and repairs radios, plus navigation, weapons control, flight control equipment.	Aptitude for electronics and computers. Strong understanding of math. Some physics, trigonometry desirable.	Repair and installation of radios, televisions, computers. Airlines, airports, manufacturers. Companies with computers.
Fuels Specialist		
Operation of fuel systems, from receipt to storage and dispersal. Quality control checks. Some computer use and bookkeeping.	Good grounding in chemistry, mathematics, general science. Attention to detail. Some outdoor work in harsh conditions.	Any petroleum related job, from oil rigs and processors to neighborhood filing station. Airports, firms with own fuel operations.
Geodetics Technician		
Maintains and updates maps. Uses telemetry and photo intelligence. Prepares target and flight maps. Stores topographic data.	Drafting, ability to use precision equipment. Great attention to detail. Algebra, trigonometry and geometry necessary. Computer use.	Mapmaker, cartographer, topographic specialist. Environmental work, resource-exploration. Any use of advanced imagery.
Intelligence Specialist		
Gathers and interprets information. Prepares maps and graphics. Analyzes and displays imagery. Writes intelligence reports.	Ability to communicate clearly verbally and in writing. Comfortable with ambiguity. Can be cleared for highest security access.	Investigator, journalist, researcher. Any job with premium on stability. Civilian law enforcement or intelligence agencies.
Munitions Specialist		
Stores and maintains explosive materials. Some oversight of shipping and distribution, plus supporting documentation.	Mechanical aptitude. Knowledge of computers helpful. Good vision, dexterity and emotional stability.	Construction work, demolitions, storage of toxic materials. Inspector. Any work requiring attention to detail.
Pavement Technician		
Constructs and maintains roads, runways. Analyzes soils, construction material. Performs erosion control. Operates heavy equipment.	Solid skills in mathematics and chemistry. Ability to read blueprints. Mechanical drawing helpful. Some computer work and writing.	Civilian work calling upon same skills – plumber, grounds keeper, bricklayer, construction worker, sheet metal worker, welder.

Sources: Profile: Life in the Armed Forces, DoD High School News Service, Norfolk, Va., and *Military Careers*, Defense Department, Washington, D.C. (1998 edition).

Marine Corps

Duties	Qualifications	Civilian Jobs
Air Defense Artillery		
Operates and maintains electrical equipment. Communicates with air-traffic controllers. Monitors computers and telemetry.	Proficient in mathematics. Comfortable with electronics and mechanical devices. Stable. Good observation and reasoning skills.	Radar operator, data processing repair, maintenance of electrical equipment, repair radios, radar, telemetry equipment.
Ammunition Handler		
Stores and maintains explosive materials. Some oversight of shipping and distribution, plus supporting documentation.	Mechanical aptitude. Knowledge of computers helpful. Good vision, dexterity and emotional stability.	Construction work, demolition, storage of toxic materials. Inspection. Any work requiring attention to detail.
Armor		
Operates and maintains heavy equipment. Interprets maps. Member of reconnaissance team and security force.	Good physical fitness. Mechanical skill, good with mathematics and communications. Good working with a team.	Operate or repair of heavy equipment. Truck mechanic. Some electrical, optical work. Security. Supervise related fields.
Combat Engineering		
Constructs, repairs and maintains roads, bridges, port facilities, pipelines, supply tanks. Some demolition.	Solid mathematical skills. Good with carpentry, mechanical challenges. Some drawing and drafting helpful.	Construction worker, heavy equipment operator, drafter, rigger, bridge repair, highway repair, lumber worker, blaster.
Communications / Electronic Warfare		
Installs, operates and maintains computers, electronics, radios, testing, measuring and calibration equipment.	Aptitude for radio and television repair. Understanding of electronics and blueprints. Eligible for highest security clearances.	Radio control room technician, radio mechanic, transmitter repair. Repair and inspect other electrical equipment.
Field Artillery		
Operates and maintains radar and meteorological equipment. Operates unique computer programs and radios.	Mathematical skills essential. Mechanical aptitude helpful. Meteorological, computer and communications skills necessary.	Surveyor, topographic drafter, cartographer, meteorologist, radio operation. General computer or radio fields.
Infantry		
Works in closely coordinated teams, requiring adaptability, stability, good verbal communications, understanding of people.	Highest state of physical fitness. Mechanical aptitude helpful. Knows how to work with people. Communicates well, handles stress.	Police, fire or security work. Dispatcher. Fitness instructor, counselor or human relations specialist. Any team-based effort.
Intelligence		
Gathers and interprets information. Some interpretation of imagery and working with POWs. Stores, displays information.	Ability to communicate clearly in word and writing. Comfortable with ambiguity. Can be cleared for highest security access.	Investigator, journalist, researcher. Any job with premium on stability. Civilian law enforcement or intelligence agencies.

Sources: Profile: Life in the Armed Forces, DoD High School News Service, Norfolk, Va., and *Military Careers*, Defense Department, Washington, D.C. (1998 edition).

Coast Guard

Duties	Qualifications	Civilian Jobs
Boatswain's Mate		
Performs basic seamanship tasks. Operates small boats, stores cargo, handles ropes. Variety of jobs aboard larger vessels.	Good physical fitness. Basic understanding of algebra and mathematics helpful. Works as part of team. Comfortable with heights.	Similar jobs with shipping companies, Merchant Marine, cruise lines. Stevedore, cargo handler, winch operator.
Gunner's Mate		
Operates and maintains missile launchers, cannon. Some work with hydraulics direction-finding gear and electrical systems.	Mechanical aptitude a must. Understanding of mathematics, electronics and optical systems good. Strong attention to detail.	Storage, maintenance of weapons and explosives. Any electrical or mechanical work. Civilian contractors. Police, fire departments.
Hull Maintenance		
Makes and installs shipboard structures, plumbing and related systems. Tests metallic materials. Inspects and stores material.	High mechanical aptitude. General knowledge of sheet metal, carpentry, plumbing. Geometry, mathematics and chemistry helpful.	Plumbing and construction work. Nuclear reactor technician. Welder. Technician in public utilities. Cruise ships.
Intelligence		
Gathers and interprets information. Prepares maps and graphics. Analyzes and displays imagery. Writes intelligence reports.	Ability to communicate clearly verbally and in writing. Comfortable with ambiguity. Can be cleared for highest security access.	Investigator, journalist, researcher. Any job with premium on stability. Civilian law enforcement or intelligence agencies.
Marine Science Technician		
Makes visual and instrumental observations of weather and sea. Performs chemical analysis, logs data. Uses precision equipment.	Algebra, mathematics, general science necessary. Uses numbers and computers to solve problems. Detail-oriented.	Oceanographer, meteorologist. Statistical clerk. Any user and maintainer of precision equipment.
Quartermaster		
Steers ship. Navigator. Oversees lookouts. Stands watch in bridge. Uses radio and navigational aids. Some maintenance.	Good vision and hearing. Ability to communicate clearly. Strong "people" skills, and understanding of electronics, mathematics.	Operation of any maritime vessel, from barge to cruise ship. Any job relying on judgment and ability to make snap decisions.
Storekeeper		
Maintains supply operation, from ordering and receiving to inventories and quality control. Uses computers and mechanical equipment.	Comfortable with computers. Able to type. Basic bookkeeping. General business studies and math. Ability to write clearly.	Any shipping or inventory operation. Invoice, purchasing agent, bookkeeper or stock control clerk.
Yeoman		
Clerical assistant. Typing, filing, uses office equipment. Tracks correspondence. May keep personnel, finance records.	General office skills. Strong English, typing, business skills. Stenography useful but not necessary. Basic computer skills.	Secretary, office clerk, office manager. Human-resources or pay clerk. Any job calling for general office skills and experience.

Sources: Profile: Life in the Armed Forces, DoD High School News Service, Norfolk, Va., and *Military Careers*, Defense Department, Washington, D.C. (1998 edition).

★ ★ Appendix G ★ ★

LOCATIONS OF MEPS CENTERS

The Military Entrance Processing Station, or MEPS, is the step that comes between the recruiter and boot camp. At MEPS, potential recruits discover if they have the physical condition to join the military. MEPS is also where recruits take aptitude tests that determine the skills and training they will be offered.

Here are the locations of MEPS facilities at the beginning of the year 2000:

Alabama: Montgomery

Alaska: Anchorage

Arizona: Phoenix

Arkansas: Little Rock

California: Los Angeles, Oakland, Sacramento, San Diego

Colorado: Denver

Florida: Jacksonville, Miami, Tampa

Georgia: Atlanta

Hawaii: Honolulu

Idaho: Boise

Illinois: Chicago

Iowa: Des Moines

Indiana: Indianapolis

Kentucky: Louisville

Louisiana: New Orleans, Shreveport

Maine: Portland

Maryland: Baltimore

Massachusetts: Boston, Springfield

Michigan: Detroit, Lansing

Minnesota: Minneapolis

Mississippi: Jackson

Missouri: Kansas City, St. Louis

Montana: Butte

Nebraska: Omaha

New Mexico: Albuquerque

New York: Albany, Buffalo, New York, Syracuse

North Carolina: Charlotte, Raleigh

North Dakota: Fargo

Ohio: Columbus

Oklahoma: Oklahoma City

Oregon: Portland

Pennsylvania: Harrisburg, Philadelphia, Pittsburgh

Puerto Rico: San Juan

South Carolina: Fort Jackson

South Dakota: Sioux Falls

Tennessee: Knoxville, Memphis, Nashville

Texas: Amarillo, Dallas, El Paso, Houston, San Antonio

Utah: Salt Lake City

Washington: Seattle, Spokane

West Virginia: Beckley

Wisconsin: Milwaukee

GLOSSARY

ASVAB. Standardized apptitude test given to potential recruits. Used to identify skills and interests. Stands for "Armed Services Vocational Aptitude Battery."

Base. One name for a military installation. Used by Navy, Air Force, Marines, and Coast Guard.

Basic Allowance for Housing (BAH). Extra money in a paycheck for active-duty people living off base. Can go to recruits at basic training whose families live off base.

Basic Allowance for Subsistence (BAS). Extra money in a paycheck when military folks don't eat in a government dining hall.

Basic Pay. The military equivalent of a salary. Everyone with the same rank and number of years of service receives the same Basic Pay.

BDU. Uniform for physical work. Stands for "battle dress uniform."

Bearing. Composure under verbal and physical pressure. Often called "military bearing."

Boot Camp. A training facility for people new to the military.

Bulkhead. Wall (Navy, Marine Corps, Coast Guard).

BX. Military department store. Stands for "base exchange."

Chain of Command. The list of people with authority over you, starting with your immediate supervisor and ending with the president of the United States.

Colors. Flag.

Command-sponsored. A term applied to spouses and children in military housing and government-paid moves. A "command-sponsored" dependent is one for whom the government will reimburse costs or authorize government housing.

Commissary. A military grocery store.

Compartment. Room (Navy, Marine Corps, Coast Guard).

CONUS. Shorthand for "continental United States," which are the states of the union, minus Alaska and Hawaii. The opposite is "OCONUS," or "outside the continental United States."

CQ. Person on duty—and awake—at night in a sleeping area. Stands for "charge of quarters."

Deck. Floor (Navy, Marine Corps, Coast Guard).

Delayed Entry Program (DEP). People agree under this program to a legal obligation to come into the military at a specific, later date, usually in exchange for attending a specific skill-related course.

Dependent. A spouse, child or another family member eligible to receive a military ID card.

Deployment. Assignment away from your home base, usually done as a member of a unit and frequently with little notice. Typically, families don't follow military folks on deployments.

Discharge. Anything involving the end of time in uniform and the return to civilian life.

Duty Station. The place you work. Usually a geographical location, such as a post, base, station, but it can be a ship.

Enlistment Contract. A formal document signed by everyone entering the military that spells out the promises made to the new recruit (assignment, training, bonuses) and the obligations assumed by the recruit (staying drug-free, serving a specific time).

Exchange. A military department store.

Furlough. Time off. It isn't counted in the tally of annual leave.

Gig Line. A vertical line extending from the edge of shirt, to the edge of belt buckle, to the edge of fly. Those three elements must be in a straight line on most uniforms.

Grade. Rank for officers.

Head. Bathroom (Navy, Marine Corps, Coast Guard).

HQ. Headquarters.

IG. A military investigator who looks at charges of wrongdoing. Short for "Inspector General."

JAG. A military lawyer. Short for "Judge Advocate General."

Leave. The military's version of vacation time. One month on active duty earns two and a half days' leave.

Liberty. Time off. It isn't counted in the tally of annual leave.

MEPCOM. The place new recruits go after leaving the recruiters and before arriving at boot camp, where physical exams and ASVAB tests are given. Short for "Military Entrants Processing Command." Also known as MEPS.

MRE. Packaged food to eat in the field. Short for "Meals, Ready to Eat."

MWR. Any recreational program or facility. Short for "Morale, Welfare and Recreation."

NCO. A mid- to senior-level enlisted person. Stands for "noncommissioned officer."

Non-Prior Service. Refers to a person who has never been in the military. Important detail for recruiters.

OCONUS. Shorthand for "outside the continental United States," which means either in a foreign country, in Alaska, or in Hawaii. Usually used in discussing rules for assignments. The opposite is "CONUS," or "continental United States."

Permanent Party. People stationed at a training base who aren't trainees.

Post. The Army's name for a military installation. Also the exact spot a military member is supposed to be, as in, "Your post is in that foxhole."

POV. Your car. Stands for "privately owned vehicle."

PX. A military department store. Stands for "post exchange."

Quarters. Where you live off duty. It can refer to a shipboard cabin, government-provided housing, or even the home you're buying off base.

Reserve Components. A way of saying "reserves and National Guard."

Sick call. A time in the morning when military clinics take patients. Also applied to any time a military member leaves work for medical purposes.

Space Available. A broad term commonly used in medical facilities and military flights. It denotes services that can be given to dependents once top-priority military needs are met.

Time in Grade. The length of time a person has held a rank.

Time in Service. The length of time someone has been in the military.

Tour of Duty. The length of an assignment to a place or job.

UCMJ. The collection of the military's criminal laws, defendants' rights, and rules for courtroom procedures. Called the "Uniform Code of Military Justice." It is the legal basis of the military punishing people for crimes like murder, rape, and robbery. It creates crimes that don't exist in civilian society, like "desertion," "conduct unbecoming an officer," and "fraudulent enlistments."

Uniform Code of Military Justice. See "UCMJ," above.

SELECTED BIBLIOGRAPHY

RECRUITING AND TRAINING

U.S. Coast Guard. *Helmsman*. Cape May, New Jersey: U.S. Coast Guard, undated.

U.S. Department of Defense. *Military Careers*. 1998 ed. Washington, D.C.: Government Printing Office, 1998.

U.S. Department of Defense High School News Service. *Profile: Life in the Armed Forces*. 1998 ed. Norfolk, Virginia: Department of Defense High School News Service, 1998.

U.S. Department of Labor. *Occupational Outlook Handbook*. 1998 ed. Washington, D.C.: Government Printing Office, 1998.

U.S. Military Entrance Processing Command. *Exploring Careers: The ASVAB Workbook*. North Chicago, Illinois: Military Entrance Processing Command, 1997.

U.S. Military Entrance Processing Command. *ASVAB 18/19: Educator and Counselor Guide*. North Chicago, Illinois: Military Entrance Processing Command, 1995.

U.S. Military Entrance Processing Command. *ASVAB 18/19: Student and Parent Guide*. North Chicago, Illinois: Military Entrance Processing Command, 1998.

U.S. Military Entrance Processing Command. *Technical Manual for the ASVAB 18/19 Career Exploration Program*. North Chicago, Illinois: Military Entrance Processing Command, 1999.

MILITARY AND VETERANS BENEFITS

Army Times Publishing Co. *Handbook for Military Living*. 1999 ed. Springfield, Virginia: Army Times Publishing Co., 1999.

Budahn, P. J. *Drawdown Survival Guide*. Annapolis, Maryland: Naval Institute Press, 1993.

Budahn, P. J. *Military Money Guide*. Mechanicsburg, Pennsylvania: Stackpole Books, 1996.

Budahn, P. J. *Reservist's Money Guide*. Mechanicsburg, Pennsylvania: Stackpole Books, 1997.

Budahn, P. J. *Veterans Guide to Benefits*. 2nd ed. Mechanicsburg, Pennsylvania: Stackpole Books, 1997.

MILITARY HISTORY

Cutler, Thomas L. *The Bluejacket's Manual*. 22nd ed. Annapolis, Maryland: Naval Institute Press, 1998.

Howarth, Stephen. *To Shining Sea: A History of the United States Navy*. Norman: University of Oklahoma Press, 1991.

Johnson, Robert Erwin. *Guardians of the Sea: History of the United States Coast Guard, 1915 to Present*. Annapolis, Maryland: Naval Institute Press, 1987.

McFarland, Stephen L. *A Concise History of the U.S. Air Force*. Washington, D.C.: Government Printing Office, 1997.

Millett, Allan R. *Semper Fidelis: The History of the United States Marine Corps*. New York: The Free Press, 1991.

U.S. Army, Center of Military History. *Army Historical Series: American Military History*. Washington, D.C.: Government Printing Office, 1969.

INDEX

ABOUT THE AUTHOR

P. J. BUDAHN is the D.C.-based spokesman for the American Legion. He is the author of *Veterans Guide to Benefits, Careers: A Military Guide,* and *Reservists Money Guide.* He has been a long-time reporter on military affairs and he is the author of top-selling books about military benefits.

355.0023 Bud
Budahn, P. J.
What to expect in the mi
litary :
$39.95 04/27/01 AGL-5219

DATE DUE

SARATOGA SPRINGS PUBLIC LIBRARY
(518) 584 7860

DEMCO